A TREASURY OF ANCIENT INDIAN TALES

A TREASURY OF ANCIENT INDIAN TALES

Swagata Deb

Rupa . Co

First Published 2007
Second Impression 2009

Published by

Rupa . Co

7/16, Ansari Road, Daryaganj
New Delhi 110 002

Sales Centres:

Allahabad Bangalooru Chandigarh Chennai
Hyderabad Jaipur Kathmandu
Kolkata Mumbai

Typeset in 12.5 Book Antiqua by
Mindways Design
1410 Chiranjiv Tower
43 Nehru Place
New Delhi 110 019

Printed in India by
Saurabh Printers Pvt. Ltd.
A-16 Sector-IV
Noida 201 301

CONTENTS

ASSORTED MYTHS

THE STORY OF HANUMAN'S CHILDHOOD

Hanuman's father was Vayu, the wind god, and his mother was a monkey named Anjana. This is the story of the miraculous way in which Hanuman was born and what he was like in his childhood.

Actually, Hanuman's mother, Anjana, was also a goddess in Indraloka—the kingdom of the gods, which is ruled by Indra. But a holy man's curse had turned her into a monkey, and she was sent to live on earth with other monkeys. Anjana remained unhappy about this.

She was the most beautiful amongst all the monkeys. But the other monkeys got fed up with her because she was so gloomy all the time. One day the queen of monkeys said to her, 'I know that you were once a goddess and you miss Indraloka. But you are a monkey now, and the most beautiful amongst us. Monkeys are such cheerful, lively creatures. You could also be like that if you accepted what you are. Be one of us and stop thinking about Indraloka! We will find a monkey-husband for you, who will make you very happy.'

The king of monkeys also tried to make her understand. 'You should be proud to be a monkey,' he said. 'We are elegant and noble. The holy man tried to turn you into an ugly creature, but he couldn't. You are so beautiful. Let's find a husband for you. You will have children who will add glory to our race.'

But these words could not make Anjana happy. 'You are very kind to show your concern,' she said, 'but I don't feel ready for marriage. I am still not used to being a monkey. And I can't forget Indraloka. That is my home and I want to go back there some day.'

So she remained sad and lonely and wandered off into the forest. When she felt tired, she lay down under the shade of a tree. The cool breeze soothed her, and she fell asleep.

The cool breeze was actually Vayu, the wind god, wandering about. He saw Anjana fast asleep and fell in love with her immediately because of her beauty. He touched her and kissed her with his most gentle breeze. Anjana woke up with a start and said, 'Who is that? Who touched me? I can't see anyone.'

'You cannot see me because I am Vayu, the wind,' said Vayu. 'But please do not be afraid. I have fallen in love with you and I want to give you a son.' 'It is cruel of you to make fun of me in this manner,' said Anjana. 'You cannot be in love with me because I am just an ugly monkey. And I don't want a son because he would look like me.'

'Yes, and what a handsome monkey he would be!' said Vayu. 'You are mistaken to think that you are ugly. You are very beautiful and your son will be as good-looking as you are. Look! Here is your son!' A god can father a child at once. Anjana looked down and saw a baby monkey on the ground nearby. Seeing her child, Anjana's motherly feelings were kindled. Its monkey face did not seem ugly to her at all. She picked it up, held it in her lap, and began to suckle it. 'I was so wrong to think that monkeys are ugly,' she thought. 'This is the loveliest baby I have ever seen. He is my child and I love him.'

Vayu smiled to see Anjana so happy. He went around the happy pair three times, blessed them and said, 'Our son will be called Hanuman, the son of wind. He will have my strength, my speed, and my power to fly across the world. He will be kind and brave. He will be a hero, who will do a lot of good in this world and make us very proud of him.'

Anjana slowly walked back to the monkey kingdom with Hanuman in her arms. She showed him proudly to the king and queen of monkeys and told them about the marvellous way in which he had been born. They were delighted to hear her story, and all the monkeys of the kingdom celebrated the birth of Hanuman.

Hanuman was brought up amongst the other monkeys by Anjana, who was now contented to be a monkey. Monkeys are said to be mischievous creatures, and so was young Hanuman. Besides, he had god-like powers and could cause a lot of destruction when he chose to be naughty. He could run and fly like the wind, as his father had said he would, and could compete with the fastest animals and birds. He spent all his time chasing them. His mother had a tough time keeping him under control. He was also very curious about new places, and his

mother never knew where he would be the next moment.

The older monkeys found Hanuman to be very annoying, because when they were having serious discussions, he would creep up behind them and tie their tails together! Or he would disturb them by letting out shrieks from a hiding place nearby.

But his godly powers also kept him protected. His mother knew that no matter what he did, he would not die. She knew that from his childhood onwards. When he was small, she had once dropped him by accident from the top of a mountain. Hanuman crashed down, thousands of feet below, landed his head on a rock, and bounced right back into her arms. The rock was smashed into a thousand pieces, but Hanuman was completely unhurt!

One day Hanuman looked at the rising sun. It was large and red, and Hanuman thought that it was a ball! 'I want to play with that ball,' he thought, and flew off straight to get it. Surya, the sun god, had never been chased before and was much alarmed. He fled from his usual place along with all the planets, but Hanuman continued to run after him. There was havoc on planet Earth. No one knew whether it was night or day. The Earth moved away from her usual orbit and there were earthquakes, avalanches and floods. People thought the world was coming to an end.

Surya was frightened to see what was happening on Earth. He went to Lord Indra, the king of all the gods, to ask for his help. Indra could be very fearsome when angry. He saw that Hanuman had gone too far this time and decided to teach him a lesson. He aimed his heaviest thunderbolt at the flying monkey and it hit him so hard that he fell back to the earth, unconscious.

Hanuman lay there, drooping and lifeless. His father Vayu was dismayed to see him like that. He wailed with grief, so much so that hurricanes blew across the world. Then he gently lifted his child and transported him to a distant cave. He then sat down beside him, feeling sad and gloomy, thinking that Hanuman was dead.

Hurricanes are bad, but it is worse if the wind comes to a stop. Since Vayu was so depressed, there was not a trace of wind in the world. All the plants began to perish from the lack of air, and the animals and human beings began to suffocate.

The gods looked down from Indraloka and were deeply concerned. 'Look at all the creatures gasping for air,' they said. 'See the plants withering. Indra is still in a bad mood and is unable to notice anything. We must go to Brahma, the greatest of the gods.'

Brahma is the creator of the universe and comes to one's rescue, when in need. When the gods approached him, he agreed to speak to Vayu. But he said to Indra, 'You must come with me and tell Vayu that you are sorry for hurting his son. He is only a young monkey after all. Don't you think that hurling your biggest thunderbolt at him was too much of a punishment?'

Indra felt sorry for what he had done and meekly followed Brahma to the cave where Hanuman lay. Vayu was sitting beside his son, dazed with grief.

'O Vayu,' said Brahma. 'The world cannot survive if you stop blowing. Indra did a mistake, but what you are doing is wrong too. You cannot punish the whole world for what Indra did to your son. Look, Indra has realised his mistake and is sorry for what he did. Forgive him and save the world with your breath.'

Vayu looked at Brahma with sadness in his eyes. 'If I have to forgive Indra, I will,' he said. 'But what about my son? Who will bring my brilliant, naughty son back to life? Without him, I don't have the heart to stir up a wind.'

Brahma smiled, and with great love he took Hanuman into his lap. He gently stroked and patted him. And then slowly, sleepily, Hanuman opened his eyes. 'You were very naughty,' said Brahma. 'Your mischief frightened the sun, rocked the earth, angered Indra, and made Vayu very sad. But you have special powers. I shall make you even more powerful by giving you nobility, kindness, and wisdom. You will grow to become the wisest of all the monkeys. You will help Rama and Sita when they are in trouble. You will add glory to the race of monkeys and will also live forever.'

Tears of joy filled the eyes of Vayu, Indra, Surya, Anjana, and all those who had been distressed by the recent incidents. Vayu stirred up a wind, and all the living creatures breathed normally again. Hanuman had learnt his lesson. He remained charming and playful, but was now considerate of others, modest and studious. And everyone loved him.

\NGA'S DESCENT

The holy river Ganges is actually a goddess. And this is the story of how she was brought down to the earth from her heavenly home.

She was the daughter of Himavat, the god of the Himalayas, and goddess Mena. The highest peaks of the Himalayas reach right up to heaven, and it was in this region that the river Ganga originally flowed. She was brought down because of Sagara, the king of Ayodhya.

Sagara had two wives, but neither of them had borne him a child. So he performed a special ceremony to pay homage to a sage called Bhrigu. Bhrigu was pleased with his devotion and granted him a boon. He said that one of Sagara's wives would give birth to a son and the other would bear a gourd, and when this gourd fell to the ground, sixty thousand sons would burst forth!

And that is exactly what happened. When Sagara's sixty thousand and one sons grew up, he became very conceited. He decided to perform the Ashwamedha Yagna. This is a sacrifice in which a horse is let loose and the owner of the horse gets to possess all the regions through which the horse passes. Sagara sent the horse to Indraloka, hoping to overthrow Indra and rule his kingdom!

When Indra realised what was happening, he turned himself into a ferocious demon, drove the horse to the underworld and left it there. The horse wandered about for some time and then started grazing near the place where the great sage Kapila was meditating.

The priest performing the Ashwamedha sacrifice got really frightened when he learnt that the horse had been driven to the underworld. This was an ominous sign and would certainly bring ruin to the kingdom. He ran to Sagara and told him what had happened.

The arrogant Sagara did not lose his confidence. 'Why do you worry?' said he. 'My men can bring back the horse from the deepest of depths.' And he commanded his sixty thousand sons to dig up the earth and bring back the horse.

Their relentless digging caused severe pain to Mother Earth. She went and complained to Lord Brahma. Lord Brahma asked her to bear the pain for some time more. 'The sons of Sagara are digging their way to their own ruin,' he said.

The sons kept digging till they reached the other side of Earth, where she is carried on the backs of huge elephants. And this was the place where the great sage Kapila lived. The sons found the horse grazing nearby. They thought that Kapila had stolen it and rushed to get hold of him in order to punish him. Kapila opened his eyes and found sixty thousand men charging at him. He was so furious that his eyes turned into balls of fire and all the sons got burnt to ashes in the intense heat of the flames.

Sagara had been waiting patiently for his sons to return with the horse. He was worried and sent his grandson Ansuman to look for them. (Ansuman's father was Sagara's son by his other wife. He led a hermit's life and was of no use in such matters.) Ansuman found his way to Kapila's ashram very easily. He just had to follow the tunnel dug by his sixty thousand uncles. When he met Kapila, his behaviour was very different from that of his uncles'. He greeted him humbly and asked him politely about what had happened to his brothers and the horse. Kapila was so charmed by the young man that he said that his uncles could be brought back to life if Ganga could be persuaded to flow over their ashes. He let Ansuman take the horse back home so that the Ashwamedha ceremony could be completed.

Sagara spent the rest of the thirty thousand years of his reign trying to find a way to bring Ganga down to the earth. But he failed. Ansuman succeeded him as king and continued the effort, but was unsuccessful. It was Sagara's great grandson, Bhagiratha, who finally managed to do this.

Bhagiratha was extremely determined by nature and could perform extraordinary feats to please the gods. In order to bring down Ganga, he fasted, stayed in one posture for years, and even walked on burning hot stones! Brahma was pleased with his devotion and agreed to let Ganga come down to the earth. However, Brahma realised that if Ganga came crashing down, with all her weight, from heaven, it might be too much for the earth to bear. So he asked Bhagiratha to pray to Shiva, so that Shiva would catch Ganga in his hair and thus prevent her great fall.

Bhagiratha then performed similar feats to please Shiva. Shiva was impressed and agreed to catch Ganga in his dense, tangled locks. Brahma then commanded Ganga to descend to the earth.

But Ganga loved her peaceful life in heaven and had no desire to flow through the earth. She was angry with Brahma and Shiva, but did not dare to disobey them. However, she decided to teach Shiva a lesson. She thought that she would cascade down to the earth and drag Shiva to the darkest region in the underworld.

So she plunged down with great force. Her waters ripped apart trees and crushed mountains. But Mount Kailash, which is the home of Lord Shiva, was too big to get affected, and Shiva was too powerful to get swept off by Ganga. He caught her in his hair as planned. His matted hair was so thick and tangled that Ganga flowed through it helplessly and was not able to find a way out.

Flowing round and round Shiva's hair, she got exhausted and her proud spirit broke. When Brahma saw that Ganga had learnt her lesson, he told Bhagiratha to perform more feats in order to

Ganga's Descent

persuade Shiva to show mercy on Ganga.

This time Bhagiratha balanced himself on the little finger of one of his hands, in a barren desert, for two hundred years! Shiva finally agreed to release Ganga from his hair. Ganga came down graciously this time and divided into several branches. Bhagiratha rode in a chariot, ahead of her, leading her down to the ashes of Sagara's sixty thousand sons.

But there were more hurdles on the way. Ganga, by mistake, flooded the place where Sage Jahnu was meditating. Jahnu was furious, and Bhagiratha had to stand on his head, submerged in water, for three hundred years to please Jahnu. Jahnu agreed to let Ganga pass, but said that she would have to flow out through his ear.

Ganga obeyed his wishes and flowed out through his ear into the sea. Her waters then sank to the underworld and reached the ashes of the dead brothers, and they were brought back to life.

Bhagiratha began to be considered as Ganga's second father because it was he who made it possible for Ganga to flow on the earth. That is why Ganga is also known as Bhagirathi.

THE SOUND OF THUNDER

Brahma, the father of the universe, created three orders of beings—gods or Devas, who lived in Indraloka, human beings or Manavas, who lived on earth, and anti-gods or Asuras, who lived in the underworld. But none of them were happy.

The Asuras were greedy, evil and violent. They made the lives of the people on earth very difficult. They were constantly plundering villages, kidnapping women, and stealing other people's belongings. They grew very rich, as a result, and the underworld overflowed with treasures. But their conquests or riches could not bring them happiness or peace of mind.

They realised that something was wrong and decided to go to Brahma to ask him what they could do to be happy.

The Manavas were even more unhappy. First of all, the Asuras were constantly troubling them. Then they were subject to the cruelties of nature. If it didn't rain, there were droughts and crops didn't grow. If it rained a lot, there were floods. All this affected their crops and cattle. Diseases caused early deaths amongst them. Besides all this, they were also quarrelsome. They were clever at making things, but did not want to share what they made. They were fond of accumulating things and were jealous of people who had more possessions.

However, they gradually realised that something was wrong. The wisest among them decided to go to Lord Brahma for advice.

One would imagine that the Devas were very blissful in heaven. They had all the luxuries anyone could desire. There were beautiful nymphs who sang and danced for them. They had fine clothes and delicate jewellery to adorn themselves with. They possessed magical powers so that they could go where they wished, change their shape as they pleased, and satisfy any desire they had. But they weren't happy either. Their riches could not bring them lasting joy. The Devas, too, decided to visit Brahma for advice.

So one day while Brahma was resting after his hard work of Creation, with all his six eyes (Brahma has three heads) closed in meditation, the Asuras, the Manavas and the Devas gathered near him. The noise of their arrival woke him up. When he opened his eyes, all of them said in a chorus, 'Oh Brahma! Our father! We are not happy. Please tell us what to do so that we can be at peace.'

Lord Brahma uttered only one word. But it was a mighty word—a word that sounded like a clap of thunder and sent waves of sound echoing through the universe. He said, 'DA!'

Then he closed his eyes and went back to sleep. The crowd that had gathered realised that he had nothing more to say. So they went back home to ponder over what Lord Brahma had said.

After much discussion and debate, the Devas were the first ones to come to a conclusion. '"DA" must stand for "*damyata*", which means "Be self-controlled",' one of them said. 'Brahma has told us to show more restraint and not seek unlimited luxuries. That will make us happier.' This made sense to all the Devas and they agreed.

The Manavas reached their own conclusion. They decided that by 'DA' Brahma had meant '*data*' or 'to give'. 'Brahma means that we should be more giving and less possessive,' said a wise man. 'We should share what we make and co-exist peacefully with each other and all the creatures of the earth.' The other Manavas agreed with him.

The Asuras thought over it for a long, long time. They finally reached the conclusion that 'DA' stood for '*dayadhwam*', which means 'Be merciful'.

'Brahma says that we should be merciful to those who are weaker than us. We should be more kind,' said one of the Asuras, and the others agreed.

So we now know the lesson Brahma taught us – that the gods should be self-controlled, human beings should be giving, and the demons should be merciful. However, it is not an easy lesson to follow. All of us fail to follow the lesson at times and therefore bring misery to ourselves and to others. That is why it still thunders at times. 'DA, DA, DA!' says the thunder, reminding us of Brahma's teachings.

AGNI TRIES TO HIDE

At the beginning of time, after Creation took place, Agni, the god of fire, hid himself. The other gods kept looking for him so that he could be of use to people.

At first he hid deep inside the earth, below the underground water. A frog who lived in these waters began to feel very uncomfortable. Agni's fire spread heat to the water and burned his skin. So he came up to the surface of the earth and complained to the gods. 'I need cool water to be healthy,' he said. 'I can't stand the boiling hot water. I know that Agni is hiding beneath. Please find him and take him to some other place. I shall now conceal myself because I don't want to be destroyed when Agni rises up through the waters.'

The frog dived back into the water and swam to a cool, secret corner far from Agni. But Agni—who was cunning and could hear every word that was uttered—had heard the frog complaining to the gods. He found the frog, although he was such a small frog hiding under a huge rock. Then he cursed him and said, 'You will have no tongue or sense of taste because you betrayed me. Now I'll go and hide somewhere else.'

The poor frog swam up to the gods again, but now he couldn't speak and tell them what had happened or where Agni was. He jumped about, opening and shutting his mouth, but it was no use. The gods realised that Agni had punished him. With great kindness they said, 'Without a tongue you may not be able to speak, but we give you the power to croak most beautifully. Its sound will be so soothing that it will put people to sleep. You will also be able to find your way in the dark and survive in barren, underground places.'

The frog hopped away happily, and the gods began to search for Agni again. Agni was now hiding in a sacred fig tree. An elephant, who loved to eat the fig tree leaves, could feel the heat the tree was radiating. He went to the gods and told them that Agni was hiding there. Agni was even angrier this time. He burst into flames and cursed the elephant. 'Your tongue will bend backwards and you will not be able to speak. I'll find some other place to hide,' he said.

Agni then entered a bamboo thicket, but the bamboo stems were too thin to conceal him and he could be seen. So he hid inside the hollow of a *sami* tree from which fire-sticks are made.

The elephant, who had been cursed by Agni, was stamping about angrily and was unable to tell the gods what had happened. Again the gods took pity on him because they knew that it was Agni's doing. They said to the elephant, 'Your tongue may be bent backwards and you may be unable to speak, but you will be able to trumpet most beautifully. Your call will lend majesty to kings, and add splendour to their armies. And you will be able to eat any kind of plant to fill your enormous tummy.'

A parrot was the next creature to betray Agni. The parrot had noticed how hot the trunk of the *sami* tree had become. He went to the gods and told them that Agni was hiding there. Agni got so angry that the tree nearly caught fire, but he controlled himself because he wanted to remain hidden. He cursed the parrot this time and took away its power of speech.

The poor parrot went to the gods. It fluttered its wings and tried to speak, but had no words to describe its sorry state. The gods understood that Agni had cursed him. 'You will not be able to speak like men,' they said. 'But your tongue will be able to produce cheerful noises – noises that sound like words, though you will not know what they mean. You will speak like a babbling child. People will be kind to you as they are towards their children. They will keep you as a pet, feed you, and teach you more new sounds.'

Agni was still hiding in the trunk of the *sami* tree. The gods knew he was there. Agni also knew that his hiding place had been discovered, but was too ashamed to come out. The gods made sticks from the twigs of the *sami* tree. Men could rub them and produce fire. Thus Agni no longer remained confined to one place. He could now be of use to men when they needed him.

Agni accepted that the other gods had greater powers than him. But he is still very short-tempered and can burst into dangerous, destructive flames when angry. He still hasn't got over the fact that his deepest hiding place was discovered by the frog. That is why his anger sometimes comes pouring out in the form of a volcano.

HOW GANESHA GOT HIS ELEPHANT HEAD

After Shiva and Parvati were married, Parvati came to Mount Kailash to stay with Lord Shiva. Lord Shiva spent most of his time with his followers or Bhutas, who were ghostly creatures. Neither Lord Shiva nor the Bhutas knew how to conduct themselves in front of women. Life was very difficult for Parvati and her friends. They could not even bathe in peace because they did not know when the men would enter the house. Moreover, Lord Shiva's guard Nandi would scold Parvati instead of obeying her commands.

One day her friends Jaya and Bijaya said to her, 'These people don't listen to you because they are

Lord Shiva's men and are scared of him. It would be nice if we had a guard of our own.' Parvati took some mud and created a boy of unbelievable beauty with it. She named him Ganesha, dressed him up in fine clothes, and gave him ornaments to wear. Then she gave him a stick and made him stand at the door. 'What shall I do here?' asked Ganesha. 'You will be our guard,' replied Parvati. 'You will not let anyone enter the house.' Then she kissed him affectionately and went for a bath.

A little while later, Lord Shiva arrived with the Bhutas. But Ganesha would not let them enter the house.

'Don't go in,' he said. 'Mother is having a bath.'

'But I am Shiva,' said Lord Shiva, taken aback.

'I don't know anyone named Shiva,' said Ganesha. 'I can't let you in.'

'But I am her husband,' said Lord Shiva, and was about to force his way in when Ganesha hit him with the stick!

Ganesha was now in deep trouble. Lord Shiva asked the Bhutas to scare him. The Bhutas had hideous faces, but Ganesha was not scared. 'My goodness! What a pretty sight you all are!' said Ganesha. 'Please stay away.'

The Bhutas did not know what to do. They were amused, angry, and a little frightened at the same time. They went to Shiva, who sent them back to frighten Ganesha. They went to Ganesha again and made scary faces at him, but Ganesha chased them away with his stick. This went on for some time. Finally, at Shiva's orders, they went and attacked Ganesha. Shiva's two guards, Nandi and Bhringi, also joined in and pulled at Ganesha's legs. Ganesha slapped them so hard and beat up the Bhutas so badly that they did not dare to attack him again.

Meanwhile, Narada had spread the news of the fight amongst the gods. All the gods, including Brahma, Vishnu, Indra, all the holy men, and all the Apsaras gathered around Shiva's house to watch the spectacle. Shiva then said to Lord Brahma, 'Could you please speak to the gods and try to make him understand?'

Lord Brahma took all the holy men with him and went to calm Ganesha down. But Ganesha thought that Lord Brahma was one more Bhuta! He pulled at his beard and tore most of it off. Lord Brahma screamed in agony. 'Please leave me alone! I haven't come to fight with you,' he said. Ganesha was not convinced. He tugged harder at Lord Brahma's beard. Then he removed the door bolt and chased him round and round with the bolt in his hand! Defeated, Lord Brahma and the holy men went back to Shiva. Then all the gods and all the Bhutas decided to combine forces and teach Ganesha a lesson.

Parvati had been watching everything. She realised that the fight that was to follow would be quite terrible, and Ganesha would not be able to ward off his enemies with just a stick and a bolt. With her powers she created two dreadful creatures and sent them to help Ganesha.

One of the creatures had such an enormous mouth that he could swallow entire mountains! And the other creature dazzled like lightning and had thousands of arms. Between the two of them, they swallowed and destroyed all the weapons that the gods aimed at Ganesha. The gods and the Bhutas were no match for Ganesha and had to flee for their lives. The gods had seen several battles, but had never been in such a trouble before. Lord Shiva and Vishnu decided that they would have to use deception to win the battle. 'I will keep Ganesha engaged by fighting with him,' Lord Vishnu said to Shiva. 'You go and kill him from behind.'

Lord Vishnu used magic to overpower the two dreadful creatures, but Ganesha was not subdued.

He hit Lord Vishnu so hard with his mace that it took some time for him to recover. With his mace, Ganesha struck down Lord Shiva's trident and his bow. When he tried to hit Lord Vishnu once again, Lord Vishnu's chakra (discus) crushed the mace to a powder. While Ganesha was busy fighting Lord Vishnu, Lord Shiva cut off Ganesha's head with a trident from behind.

Parvati's sorrow knew no bounds. Angry with the gods for having killed her son, she used her powers once more. A thousand ghostly creatures came to life and started destroying the universe. They beat up all the gods and broke Shiva's back. It was the darkest hour for all Creation.

The gods knew that the only way to save the world was to pray to Parvati, but they were afraid of approaching her. So they said their prayers from a distance and implored her to stop the destruction. Parvati was pacified at last. 'I will forgive you if you bring my Ganesha back to life,' She said. 'And I want Ganesha to hold the highest position amongst all the gods. People should pray to him first, before they pray to any other god.'

'We have to listen to her,' said Shiva. 'We don't have a choice.' The gods were relieved. All they had to do now was to revive Ganesha. But there was one more problem. Ganesha's head was nowhere to be found! 'Start praying to his body,' said Shiva. 'And some of you go to the north. Behead the first person you find there and bring back his head. We shall attach it to Ganesha's body.'

A number of gods rushed towards the north at once. The first creature that they saw was a beautiful white elephant. This elephant's head was then attached to Ganesha's body. Prayers were chanted and Ganesha revived. Parvati was overjoyed to get her son back, and the world was saved.

Now you know why Ganesha has the head of an elephant and why, before the start of any ceremony, prayers are said to Ganesha first.

DEVAS AND ASURAS

AGASTYA RISHI DRINKS UP THE OCEAN

The gods in Indraloka were immortal, but they still had trouble keeping the Asuras in check. The Kaleya clan of Asuras were particularly troublesome. Their leader, Vrittasura, was so powerful that the gods trembled whenever they heard his name. They felt so helpless that they finally went to Lord Brahma to ask him for advice.

'I will tell you how you can defeat Vrittasura,' said Lord Brahma. 'There is a great sage named Dadhichi. Go to him and ask him for a boon. He will certainly grant you a wish. Then you must say to him, "For the good of mankind, please donate your bones." Dadhichi will gladly die to save the world. You will then have to make a deadly weapon named Vajra from his bones. The weapon will be hexagonal in shape and will produce a deafening sound. Indra will find it very easy to kill Vritta with it.'

So the gods went to Rishi Dadhichi's ashram at the bank of the river Saraswati. When they saw him, they touched his feet to show respect and made their request. 'I will not let you go back empty-handed,' said Dadhichi. 'Your wish will be fulfilled.' As he said this, his soul left his body and made its way to heaven. The gods took his bones to Lord Vishwakarma, the god of weapons and tools.

'We have brought the bones of Rishi Dadhichi so that you can make Vajra for us,' they said to him. 'Could you please make the weapon quickly because Indra needs it to kill Vrittasura.'

Lord Vishwakarma was only too happy to make the deadly weapon Vajra, and when the weapon was made, Indra was overjoyed to hold it in his hands. Then a fierce battle took place between the gods and the Asuras. The Kaleyas attacked with all their might and all the gods fled from the battlefield. The angry Vrittasura grew in size till he was as big as a mountain. When Indra saw what was happening, he fainted with fright.

No one knows what could have happened had Lord Vishnu not come to his rescue. When he saw Indra in this sorry state, he donated some of his own strength to him. Invigorated with renewed strength and power, Indra felt fearless once more.

When Indra went to the battlefield, carrying Vajra in his hand, Vrittasura let out a terrible cry. Trembling with fear, Indra hurled the Vajra at him, closed his eyes, and ran as fast as he could. He did not even wait to see where the Vajra fell, but went and hid inside a pond.

The deadly weapon had killed Vrittasura. The gods now started killing the Asuras with great enthusiasm, singing praises of Indra. Having lost their leader, the Asuras felt weak and helpless. Unable to stand up to the gods, they ran and took shelter under the ocean. There they held meetings and decided to destroy the whole world. Some of the more intelligent Asuras formulated a plan that would help them wipe out the world.

The earth gets its beauty and glory from the yagnas and prayers performed by holy men. So they decided to kill all the Brahmanas and priests. With the priests gone, there would be no one to offer prayers to the gods. The world would lose its lustre and soon get destroyed.

The Kaleyas began to carry out their plan. They would hide under the ocean during the daytime. At night they would emerge from their hiding place and kill the priests and holy men. Then they would get back to the bottom of the ocean before daybreak. In this manner they killed one hundred and ninety seven holy men from Rishi Vashishtha's ashram, a hundred priests from Rishi Chyavan's ashram, and twenty people from Rishi Bhardwaj's hermitage. People lost count of the number of people they killed in the other ashrams.

People on earth stopped travelling in fear of the Asuras. Some ran to the mountains and hid in caves. Some who were cowardly died of fright! Some of the brave men formed groups and hunted for the Asuras, but they were nowhere to be found.

The gods were worried to see what was happening on the earth. Together they went to Vishnu and said, 'You are our saviour. Please protect us from the unknown enemy.'

Lord Vishnu told them that the Kaleya Asuras were responsible for what was happening on the earth. 'After Indra killed Vrittasura, the Kaleyas went and hid under the ocean,' he said. 'They come out at night, create havoc, and go back to their hiding place before sunrise. And as long as they have the ocean cover, we can do nothing to stop their atrocities.'

'The only way to defeat them is to dry up the ocean. I know a man with remarkable powers. He has the capacity to drink up the entire ocean. His name is Rishi Agastya. He is our only hope.'

The gods thanked Lord Vishnu and then went to Rishi Agastya's ashram. When Rishi Agastya heard everything, he was ready to drink up the entire ocean. As Agastya made his way to the ocean, people could not sit still at home. Devas, Gandharvas, Yakshas, Rakshasas, all followed him to watch the amazing spectacle. When he reached the ocean, Rishi Agastya said, 'I am now going to drink up all the water. You must hurry up and finish your work.' And then he started drinking up all the water in the ocean, making a tremendous noise as he sipped the water.

The gods had not seen such an extraordinary sight before. They began to chant Rishi Agastya's name while he performed this incredible task. Soon the ocean dried up and the gods found that the ocean bed was teeming with Asuras.

They had now lost their protective cover, and the gods attacked them with all their strength. A large number of Asuras got killed. Only a few lucky ones managed to escape to the underworld. The gods thanked Agastya. 'We were saved because of you,' they said to him. 'We will always remember you and honour you for this deed. Could you please fill up the ocean again?'

'I won't be able to do that,' replied Rishi Agastya. 'I have already digested all the water! You will have to think of some other way to fill up the ocean.'

When the gods approached Brahma, he said that in due course Ganga would descend from heaven and her waters would fill up the ocean. Years later, Ganga came down to the earth because of King Bhagiratha's penance, and the story of how she came down is narrated in 'Ganga's Descent' in this book.

MAHISHASURA'S DEFEAT

Once upon a time there lived a terrible Asura. He was named Mahishasura because he used to disguise himself as a buffalo. 'Mahisha' in Sanskrit means buffalo.

The gods were unable to keep him in check. They fought with him for one hundred years but lost the battle in the end. Mahishasura drove them all out of heaven and became the ruler of the universe!

The gods didn't know what to do. They took Lord Brahma with them and approached Lord Shiva and Vishnu. 'We are in a sorry state because of Mahishasura,' they said. 'He has defeated us in a battle and driven us out of our homes. We have no one to turn to but you, our Lords.'

When they heard about Mahishasura's deeds, Lord Vishnu and Lord Shiva grew very angry. Their anger caused their bodies to glow with an intense light. The light was so bright that it looked as though a huge mountain of fire had engulfed heaven and hell! Slowly the light took the form of the beautiful goddess Durga.

All the gods were overjoyed to see her. They presented her with weapons. Vishnu gave her his chakra, Shiva his trident. The other gods gave her a disc, a sword, an axe, a conch, a mace, a discus, a rope, and bows and arrows. Some gods gave her robes. Others gifted armour and ornaments to her. Himalaya presented her with an enormous lion, which she could ride on.

The goddess had a thousand hands, which spread in all possible directions. Her crown pierced a hole in the sky. The earth buckled under her weight. Heaven and hell trembled at the sound of her bow. Armed with a thousand weapons in her thousand hands, she let out a cry that caused the universe to quiver. The Asuras also heard her cry and came running.

The battle that followed was not ordinary in any way. Mahishasura's commanders were as fearsome as Mahishasura himself. Mahishasura took all his commanders and millions of Asuras with him to fight the goddess. They hurled countless spears and arrows at her, but she was quite unharmed by them. Every time she breathed out, thousands of ghosts appeared from somewhere and beat up all the Asuras. Her lion also scratched and bit the Asuras. And with a thousand weapons in her thousand hands, the goddess ripped the Asuras apart and killed them. Slowly Mahishasura's commanders died. Some were killed by the goddess, some by her lion.

When he saw what was happening, Mahishasura could no longer stay still. He tossed his horns, twirled his tail, and came charging at the ghosts. The ghosts ran as fast as they could, but were unable to escape. After slaying the ghosts, Mahishasura went for the goddess' lion. As he ran, his tail caused huge waves in the ocean, his horns scattered the clouds in the sky, and his breath blew away small hills and mountains!

At this point the goddess aimed an enchanted weapon at him that tied him up so tightly that it was impossible for him to move. But Mahishasura knew magic. In the twinkling of an eye, he turned himself into a lion and bit and scratched his way out. Goddess Durga aimed at the lion, but suddenly there was no lion to be seen. Mahishasura had turned into

a man carrying a sword. When Durga killed the man, he changed into an elephant and lifted Durga's lion with his trunk. Durga cut up the elephant's trunk with her sword, and the elephant turned into a buffalo again.

With one leap Goddess Durga landed on the back of the buffalo and pierced it with her spear. Mahishasura was forced to come out of the buffalo. But his spirits were still high. He started fighting when he was halfway out of the buffalo!

The fight did not continue for too long because very soon the goddess beheaded the Asura with her spear.

All the gods and goddesses rejoiced at Mahishasura's defeat and sang praises of Durga. Goddess Durga said that they could ask for anything they desired. 'We have nothing to wish for,' said the gods. 'Now that Mahishasura is dead, we can live in peace. Only promise us that you will appear whenever we are in trouble.'

Goddess Durga assured them that she would come and help them whenever they were in need. They would only have to call out to her.

And then she vanished into thin air. It was to Goddess Durga that Rama prayed when he had to defeat Ravana.

THE STORY OF KACHA

Long long ago, the gods in heaven were not immortal and lived in constant fear of the Asuras. The unfortunate part was that when wounded in battles, the gods would die, but not the Asuras. The Asuras' teacher Shukra knew the Sanjivani mantra, which could bring the dead back to life. Brihaspati, the teacher of the gods, did not have the knowledge of Sanjivani.

First of all, the Asuras were more in number. Moreover, with the mantra, they were practically invincible. The gods thought that this was extremely unfair and decided to somehow learn the Sanjivani mantra.

With this thought in mind, they approached Kacha, the eldest son of Brihaspati. 'O Kacha! We have come to you because we are greatly troubled,' said the gods. 'You will have to do us a favour.'

Kacha bowed to show his respect to the gods and very graciously said, 'If the task is within my capabilities, I shall certainly do it. What is it that you want me to do?'

'Shukra, the son of Bhrigu, has the knowledge of Sanjivani. We want you to go to him and obtain this knowledge,' said the gods.

'I'll go right now and learn the mantra,' said Kacha. Shukracharya lived with Vrishparva, who was the king of the Asuras. Kacha took leave of the gods and went to visit him at his abode.

Shukra was seated next to Vrishparva when Kacha reached there. Kacha touched Shukra's feet to show him respect and said, 'I am Kacha, the grandson of Angira and the son of Brihaspati. I have come here to be your student. If you accept me as your pupil, I will study under your guidance for the next one thousand years.'

Brihaspati was Brahma's grandson and so was Shukra. That made Kacha his distant nephew. Kacha's pleasing manners won Shukra over. 'I greatly respect your father,' said Shukra. 'I will gladly accept you as my student.'

Thus Kacha became Shukra's pupil and started living in his house. Shukra had great affection for him, and his daughter Devayani grew completely dependent on him. Getting flowers for her, helping her with her work, singing and dancing with her for her amusement were some of Kacha's principal tasks.

But the Asuras were not happy with the situation. They suspected that Kacha had come to steal the knowledge of Sanjivani and decided to kill him in order to prevent him from learning the powerful mantra.

One day, when Kacha took Shukracharya's cows to the forest, the Asuras grabbed him, cut him up into pieces, and fed him to the dogs! At sunset, all the cows returned home, but not Kacha. Devayani grew worried. She said to Shukra, 'Father, the sun has set. The sacred fire has been lit. The cows have returned home, but Kacha has not come back. I fear greatly that he is dead. And without Kacha, I have no wish to live either.'

'Why are you afraid?' said Shukra. 'Kacha will come back right now. I will bring him back to life.'

Then he started chanting the Sanjivani mantra for Kacha. Kacha was revived and he returned home. 'What took you so long?' asked Devayani.

Kacha told her what had happened. 'I got tired picking firewood. So I lay down under a Banyan tree,' he said. 'As I was resting, some Asuras came and asked me who I was. I told them that I was Kacha, the son of Brihaspati. Then they cut me up into pieces and fed me to the dogs, laughing as they did so. I was brought back to life by your father's mantra.'

Another day, when Kacha went to fetch flowers for Devayani, the wicked Asuras killed him again, crushed his body to powder, and tossed it into the sea. Once again Devayani spoke to her father and he resurrected him using the mantra.

Undeterred, the Asuras killed Kacha for the third time, and this time they took extra care to make sure that Shukra would not be able to revive him.

Shukracharya used to drink sura. Those who drink sura tend to become careless at times. The Asuras knew this. They burnt Kacha's body and mixed his ashes in Shukra's sura. Shukra drank up the sura without realising what was mixed in it.

Devayani started crying once more. Her father was not so enthusiastic about reviving Kacha this time. 'Bringing him back to life serves no purpose,' he said. 'The Asuras won't let him live. Please don't cry, my dear daughter. Why are you feeling so bad for such an ordinary man?'

'He is the grandson of Angira and the son of Brihaspati. He himself is so well-read and pious. Kacha is no ordinary man.' replied Devayani. 'I love him father. If he dies, I will also kill myself.'

When Shukra heard these words, he grew very angry with the Asuras. 'The Danavas are killing my pupil again and again. They shall be suitably punished,' he said. And he started reciting the Sanjivani mantra for Kacha.

As he uttered Kacha's name, he could hear a faint reply from his own tummy! Taken aback, he asked Kacha, 'How did you enter my stomach?'

'The Asuras stirred me into your sura and you drank me up,' replied Kacha.

'O my God!' exclaimed Shukra. 'What have I done! How will I ever revive Kacha? I will have to die to bring Kacha back to life because he has to tear his way out of my stomach!'

When Devayani heard this, she said, 'I cannot live without either of you. You will have to decide what to do.'

Shukra thought for some time and said to Kacha, 'I will teach you the Sanjivani mantra, so that you can bring me back to life after you come out of my tummy.'

Shukracharya then taught Kacha the Sanjivani mantra. Kacha emerged from Shukra's tummy and then revived Shukra. When Shukra was reborn, he said, 'This unfortunate incident happened because I drank sura. Henceforth, Brahmanas should not be allowed to touch this vile stuff. If any Brahmana drinks sura, he shall be completely ruined.'

Then he scolded the Asuras so badly that they did not dare to harm Kacha again. One thousand years went peacefully by.

At the end of the thousand years, when it was time for Kacha to take leave of Shukracharya and return home, Devayani said to him, 'I love you. Marry me and take me home with you.'

'I respect you as much as I respect your father. Since your father is my teacher, he is also like my father. I consider you as an elder sister. Please do not talk to me in this manner.'

When Kacha saw that Devayani was saddened by his words, he tried his best to explain his feelings to her. Finally he said, 'These were some of the happiest years of my life. With your permission, I wish to return home. Please bless me so that I can reach home safely. Think of me at times and do take good care of my teacher.'

However, these words failed to pacify Devayani. In her grief, she cursed Kacha. 'Since you have deserted me, you will not be able to use the knowledge of Sanjivani to revive people.'

'I may not be able to use the mantra myself,' said Kacha. 'But I can teach the mantra to others who will be able to use it. Since you have cursed me, I shall curse you too. No holy man's son will ever marry you.'

With these words, Kacha departed. The gods were overjoyed to see him again. With the knowledge of Sanjivani, several gods were brought back to life. But the gods were not fully satisfied. They thought that it would be better still if they were immortal and did not die at all. Their next aim was to search and find the heavenly nectar that would grant them immortality. If you want to know how they found it, you will have to read the story of the Kurma Avatara in this book.

THE TEN AVATARAS OF VISHNU

Of all the gods in Hindu mythology, the three most important ones are Lord Brahma, Lord Vishnu, and Lord Shiva. Lord Brahma is the creator of the universe, Lord Vishnu is the preserver, and Lord Shiva is the destroyer.

Lord Vishnu was born nine times on earth to save the world from destruction. According to mythology, he will be born once more. These incarnations of Vishnu are known as Avataras.

Lord Vishnu took the form of a fish in Matsya Avatara, and a tortoise in Kurma Avatara. He appeared as a boar in Varaha Avatara, a half-lion half-man in Nrisimha Avatara, and a dwarf in Vamana Avatara. Parashurama, Rama, Krishna and Balarama are Avataras of Vishnu in the human form. Gautama Buddha, too, is considered by some to be an incarnation of Vishnu. At the end of the Kali Yuga, or the present times, Vishnu will appear as the Kalki Avatara and save the world.

THE MATSYA AVATARA

Pralaya or Doomsday was close at hand, and Lord Brahma was fast asleep. A powerful Asura named Hayagriva crept up to him and stole the Vedas, which had slipped out of Lord Brahma's lips.

When Lord Vishnu discovered what had happened, he wondered what to do. Pralaya was soon to follow, and the Vedas would be lost for the next cycle of Creation, unless they could be recovered in some way.

Vishnu noticed Sage Satyavrata, who was doing penance by surviving on water alone. He was offering water to the gods. Vishnu immediately took the form of a fish. As Satyavrata scooped out water from the flowing river, he noticed a tiny fish in his water. When he tried to put the fish back into the river, the fish spoke. 'Please don't put me back into the river,' it begged. 'The big fish will eat me up.' Satyavrata took pity on him and put him in his kamandalu, a small vessel containing water.

But overnight the fish grew too big for the kamandalu.The next morning it requested the sage to put him in a bigger vessel. Satyavrata obeyed his wishes, but soon the fish became too big for the larger vessel too. Once again the fish asked Satyavrata to find a suitable place for it. Satyavrata emptied the contents of the vessel into a large pond nearby. In very little time, the fish grew as large as the pond and filled it up. He asked Satyavrata to place him in a large and deep lake now. Although Satyavrata put it in several lakes, each larger than the previous one, the fish simply grew bigger and bigger and kept asking for more and more space.

Finally, Satyavrata got annoyed and decided to put the fish in the ocean. When he took him to the ocean and was about to place him there, the fish said, 'O Sage! Please do not leave me here, I beg you. I will be swallowed by all the monstrous creatures that live in the ocean.' Satyavrata's suspicions were now roused. He could not understand how a fish could

grow so big in a single day and yet be afraid to live in the ocean. In a flash the truth dawned on him. He understood that the fish was actually Vishnu.

Satyavrata immediately went down on his knees and prayed to Vishnu. He asked him why he had appeared in the form of a fish. Vishnu explained everything to his devotee. 'In another week it will be Doomsday. The ocean will rise and submerge the entire universe. At that time, you will see a big boat approaching you. You must collect all the plants, all the seeds, and all the animals needed for the next cycle of Creation. Get into the boat. The Saptha Rishis, or the seven wise sages, will also be there with you. Also take Vasuki, the king of serpents, and wait for me.'

Then the fish left to fulfil its mission. Hayagriva, the Asura, saw the colossal fish approaching him and was overcome by fear. He held the Vedas tightly in his mouth. But soon the divine fish killed him and retrieved the Vedas. Then he returned them to Lord Brahma, who would need them when it was time to start the process of Creation again.

Soon after, the Deluge set in. Rain poured down from immense clouds in the sky. The ocean swelled and engulfed the earth. On the rising waters, a boat appeared. Sage Satyavrata, the Saptha Rishis, and all forms of living creatures got on to the boat and found refuge there. The gigantic fish, now golden in colour and with a magnificent horn, approached them. The fish ordered that the boat be tied to its horn, using Vasuki as a rope.

As the boat floated safely on the rising waters, Lord Vishnu taught the Rishis the highest form of truth. This collection of truth has been compiled in the 'Matsya Purana'. And this is how all forms of life were preserved by Lord Vishnu for the next cycle of Creation.

THE KURMA AVATARA

Sage Durvasa was very hot-tempered. Once he got so angry with the gods that he cursed all of them, and their entire race was threatened because of the power of his curse. This is the story of what actually happened.

All the kings of the earth had gathered for an important meeting. Sage Durvasa had been invited so that they could honour him with a garland of flowers. Durvasa was very happy. After the meeting, he carried the garland to heaven. On his way he wondered which god he would present it to.

Finally he decided to give it to Indra. Indra received it with a great show of humility and gratitude, but actually he disliked Durvasa, as did all the other gods. As soon as Durvasa left, Indra gave it to one of his elephants to play with.

At this point Durvasa remembered something that he had forgotten to say to the gods. When he returned to heaven, he found that the garland had been trampled and crushed by the playful elephant. Durvasa was so enraged that he cursed not just Indra, but all the other gods as well. He said that the gods would lose their divine strength and become as weak as the mortals.

This was a marvellous opportunity for the Asuras. Their king Bali made preparations for a massive attack on the kingdom of heaven. The gods, who had been weakened by Durvasa's curse, were so alarmed by the prospect of a war that they went to Shiva to ask him for his help.

However, Shiva said that he did not have the power to nullify Durvasa's curse and sent them to Brahma instead. Brahma, in turn, passed on the formidable task to Vishnu.

When Indra and the other gods reached Vishnu, they found him fast asleep. He was settled very comfortably on the massive snake Ananta, whose coils formed his bed. The gods sang in chorus and chanted all his one thousand names, and Vishnu finally woke up. 'What brings you here?' he asked the gods.

The gods told him all about Durvasa's curse and how it had weakened them. They also informed him about the Asuras' imminent attack.

Vishnu thought deeply and then said, 'Your energies will be restored only if you drink from the sea of milk that surrounds me because it contains the divine nectar of immortality. But at present it is too mild to be effective. It has to be churned and infused with energy. You will not be able to churn it in your present sorry state. And an ordinary churning stick won't do. The entire Mount Mandara has to be lifted and whirled around. The only beings who can perform this task are the Asuras, who are your sworn enemies.'

The plan seemed so impossible that the gods felt confused and dejected. But Vishnu had an idea. Maybe the Asuras could be persuaded to help with the churning in return for a share of the divine nectar.

'But if we let that happen, the Asuras will become immortal,' objected Indra. 'Do you think that beings who are already so evil and vindictive should be given additional power and strength? They will then become a threat not only to us but to the entire universe.'

'I shall solve that problem when the time comes,' said Vishnu. Seeing that there was no other way, the gods made peace with the Asuras and asked for their help in churning the ocean. The Asuras were eager to help because the prospect of immortality was very exciting. They uprooted the entire Mount Mandara at one go and collected all kinds of herbs and spices to garnish the sea of milk because the Asuras did not like bland food.

The gods caught Vasuki, the king of all serpents, who lived in the underworld. They coiled him around the mountain with the little strength that they still possessed. Vasuki was to be used as a churning rope. When things were ready, Vishnu asked the gods to stay near the head of the snake and the Asuras near the tail. This was a trick, because as soon as he said that, the Asuras wanted to be near the head of the snake; and this was where Vishnu wanted them to be. Vishnu agreed to their demand and ordered them to start churning.

'The gods can pull first,' said Bali tauntingly, 'because if we start pulling, you will all fall down!' So the gods gathered all their strength and pulled the tail of Vasuki. Slowly the mountain turned. Then it was the Asuras' turn to pull. The mountain rotated much faster in the opposite direction when they pulled.

Churning the ocean would have been difficult for the gods because of their reduced strength. The Asuras were much stronger than the gods. However, the gods were invigorated by the fresh ocean breezes that blew at Vasuki's tail end. The Asuras, on the other hand, were weakened by the hot, poisonous breath of the snake. Their powers were now balanced, and the churning proceeded smoothly and effectively.

Mount Mandara was too heavy to be used as a churning stick for long. It started to sink to the bottom of the ocean. The churning would have come to a halt had the mountain slipped out of the snake's hold. But Vishnu was able to solve this problem too. He turned himself into a giant tortoise, or the Kurma Avatara, dived into the ocean, swam beneath the mountain, and supported it on his back.

The churning could now continue without hindrance, and soon the ocean was bubbling and spewing milky froth.

Days went by. Then all of a sudden the sky was filled with a soft white light, and the moon, with its smiling round face, appeared from beneath the ocean.

After sometime a beautiful lotus rose from the bottom of the ocean. Seated in the lotus was goddess Lakshmi. Her beauty filled the three worlds with heavenly light.

Everyone churned the ocean with even more enthusiasm now. Out rose a horse named Uchchashravah and a glittering gem called Kaustav. After some time, Dhanvantari, the god of medicines, appeared from beneath the ocean, carrying a white receptacle in his hands. The receptacle contained the heavenly nectar Amrit.

'It's ours! It's ours!' cried the gods, when they saw the Amrit. A white elephant named Airavat, which had four tusks, rose next from the ocean. 'It is mine,' said Indra, and it was given to him.

But then a deadly poison Kalkut rose from the ocean. Its scent was so powerful that everyone in the universe nearly fainted. 'What shall we do now?' Brahma asked Lord Shiva. 'All the creatures will surely die.' To save the world, Lord Shiva drank up the poison. The poison was so strong that his neck turned blue. That is why Shiva is also known as Neelkantha or the Blue-Necked One.

Meanwhile, the Asuras had snatched the Amrit from the gods and run away with it. The gods did not have the strength to fight the Asuras and win it back. They felt very dejected because they had toiled so hard to obtain the potion.

It was again Vishnu who came to their rescue. Disguised as a beautiful woman, he approached the Asuras. When the Asuras saw the woman's lovely face, they could not take their eyes off her. They stared at her with their mouths wide open and unblinking eyes. When this ethereal beauty asked them for a portion of the heavenly Amrit in order to partake of it, they gave it to her as though it was the most natural thing for them to do. And that is how the gods managed to obtain the heavenly nectar with the help of Lord Vishnu.

THE VARAHA AVATARA

After the end of Pralaya (Doomsday), from which Lord Vishnu saved the creatures of the earth by taking the form of a fish, it was the beginning of a new era. Lord Brahma was busy with the task of Creation. Mother Earth was being tossed about by turbulent waves. Finally she was pushed to the bottom of the ocean. Lord Brahma was worried. He would have to bring Mother Earth up, out of the deluge. He prayed to Lord Vishnu for help. 'O Lord, please come to my rescue and recover Mother Earth from the bottom of the ocean,' he said. As he prayed, a tiny white boar, smaller than his thumb, emerged from Vishnu's nostrils. Lord Brahma gazed at it in amazement. The boar grew in size and in seconds became as large as an elephant. But it didn't stop growing. It grew till it was as vast as a mountain.

The boar's colour was that of a dark cloud, and its roar was like the sound of thunder. Its tusks were white, sharp, and fearsome. Fire flashed from its eyes like lightning, and it was as radiant as the sun. Its body was smooth and beautiful. It strode like a mighty lion. Lord Brahma realised that it was Vishnu himself who had taken the form of a boar.

With a terrifying roar the boar leaped into the air, pierced through the clouds, and dived deep into the ocean. He reached the bottom of the ocean and went in search of Mother Earth. He found her at the other end of the ocean bed. He dug his tusks into the ocean bed, lifted her on to it, and started making his way to the surface.

Meanwhile, an Asura named Hiranyaksha had become very powerful. He had prayed to Lord Brahma and had obtained many boons. All the gods were so frightened of him that they went into hiding! Hiranyaksha was disappointed. He wanted to fight the gods so that he could show off his powers. He went to Varuna, the god of waters, and implored him to fight. Lord Varuna knew that he was no match for the Asura. So he refused very politely. 'I am too old to fight,' he said. 'Lord Vishnu is the only god who can match your capabilities. Please urge him to fight.'

Hiranyaksha then went in search of Lord Vishnu. He learnt from Sage Narada that Vishnu was now rising from the ocean, carrying Mother Earth on his tusk. The Asura dived into the ocean. When he spotted Lord Vishnu, he said, 'Hey beast! Let Mother Earth alone, and come and fight with me.' Vishnu ignored the Asura's taunts and continued with his task. When he reached the surface of the ocean, he placed Mother Earth in her original place and blessed her. 'May you fit into the divine order,' he said.

Then he turned to Hiranyaksha, ready to face him in battle. Hiranyaksha charged at the boar with all his strength. The boar warded off his attack and fought him with a mace. They were engaged in a furious battle when Lord Brahma made an appearance. 'Twilight is approaching and soon the Asura will become even more powerful. Slay him as quickly as you can,' said Lord Brahma to the boar.

Hiranyaksha heard what Lord Brahma had said. In a fit of anger, he hurled his mace at the boar, who caught it with the ease of a child catching a ball. Hiranyaksha now started hitting him on his chest with powerful fists. The boar, in turn, landed a blow behind Hiranyaksha's ear, and the Asura fell down dead.

Brahma and the other gods sang praises of the Lord for having saved the world once more.

THE NRISIMHA AVATARA

There was a great demon named Hiranyakashipu. His brother Hiranyaksha had just been killed by Vishnu, who had taken the shape of a huge boar. This filled Hiranyakashipu with rage. He was determined to conquer the entire universe. To achieve this end, he performed several austerities. His penance was so severe that all the gods started feeling insecure. They went to Lord Brahma and requested him to somehow put an end to the Asura's penance. Lord Brahma descended from heaven, and in order to pacify Hiranyakashipu, he asked him what he wanted.

'Please grant me the wish that I may not be killed by any living being created by you or by any weapon,' said Hiranyakashipu, 'that I will not die inside or outside a house, during the day or at night, on the ground or in the sky, and that no animal or human being is able to kill me. I wish to rule over all the gods and the living things. I also wish to acquire mystical powers.'

Lord Brahma granted him all his wishes. Hiranyakashipu immediately went and conquered all the planets and defeated all the gods. Then he moved into Indra's luxurious palace in Indraloka. Intoxicated by his own power, he ruled over the entire universe with great cruelty.

At this time, his queen Kayadhu gave birth to a son, who was named Prahlada. Even as a small boy Prahlada was brimming with virtue because he was a true devotee of Lord Vishnu. Determined to understand the Absolute Truth, he had complete control over his mind and senses. He was kind to all living creatures and befriended them. He was humble and completely free from pride that might have arisen from his education, riches, beauty and noble birth.

Hiranyakashipu wanted his son to be a powerful demon, but all that Prahlada wanted was to serve Lord Vishnu. One day Hiranyakashipu placed him on his lap and affectionately said, 'My dear child, please tell me what you have learnt in school.' Fearlessly, Prahlada replied, 'I have learnt to admire Him, who is without any beginning, middle or end, the One who cannot be diminished or enhanced, who is the imperishable Lord of the world and the cause of all causes.'

Aghast, Hiranyakashipu flung Prahlada from his lap onto the ground. 'Take him away and kill him at once!' he screamed at the servants. However, Prahlada sat quietly and meditated, and the demon's weapons had no effect on him.

Seeing this, Hiranyakashipu was afraid. He now thought of various means to kill his son. His servants threw Prahlada underneath an elephant's feet; they placed him in the midst of poisonous snakes; cursed him using powerful spells; and pushed him down a hilltop. They gave him poison to drink; they starved him, exposed him to severe cold, fire, wind and water. Hiranyakashipu even sent his sister Holika to set him on fire, but she got burnt instead. Throughout these trials, Prahlada remained utterly calm and absorbed in the thoughts of Lord Vishnu. He thus managed to stay unharmed. Hiranyakashipu was completely frustrated and did not know what to do next.

'You say that your god is superior to me,' he said to Prahlada. 'Then where is he? If he is present everywhere, why is he not present in this pillar? Do you think he is present in this pillar?'

'Yes,' replied Prahlada, 'He is there.'

Hiranyakashipu grew angrier. 'I am going to chop off your head right now,' he said. 'Let your god come and protect you. I want to see him!' Hirayakashipu drew his sword, got up, and struck his fist against the pillar.

From within the pillar emerged a heavenly creature. It was Lord Vishnu in the form of Nrisimha, who was half-man and half-lion. His burning eyes, his shining mane, and his deadly teeth made him look most fearsome. Coming out of the pillar, he attacked Hiranyakashipu.

Finally at twilight, Nrisimha captured Hiranyakashipu. He placed him on his lap at the doorway of the assembly hall, ripped him apart, and killed him. Then he flung him aside and destroyed an entire army of Hiranyakashipu's followers.

Nrisimha was able to kill Hiranyakashipu without breaking any of Lord Brahma's promises. Hiranyakashipu was killed at the doorway, which was neither inside nor outside the palace. It did not happen on land or in the sky, but on Nrisimha's lap. It was neither day nor night but twilight when this happened. Nrisimha was half-man and half-beast, and the Asura was not killed by any weapon, but by god's own hands.

With the Asura dead, all the beings in the universe heaved a huge sigh of relief. Prahlada offered his prayers to the Lord in a voice that trembled with love and devotion.

THE VAMANA AVATARA

Prajapati Daksha's daughters, Diti and Aditi, were both married to the great sage Kashyap. Diti became the mother of the Asuras and Aditi the mother of the gods.

Diti's son Hiranyaksha was killed by Vishnu in the shape of a giant boar, and his brother Hiranyakashipu by Vishnu's half-man half-lion Avatara, Nrisimha. Hiranyakashipu's great grand-son, Bali, was extremely powerful, and he conquered the whole world. Thereafter, he attacked the gods. The war between the gods and the Asuras continued for a thousand years. The Asuras emerged victorious and Bali became the ruler of all the three worlds. The gods, who were driven out of heaven, started living on earth after assuming human forms.

Aditi was extremely unhappy to see her sons in such a sorry state. So she went to a forest to pray to Lord Vishnu in solitude. The Asuras set the forest on fire to disturb Aditi's meditation. Although the whole forest burned down, Aditi was saved because she was protected by Vishnu. After a thousand years, Vishnu appeared in front of her and asked her to make a wish.

Aditi wished that her sons should regain their past glory and become the rulers of heaven once more. At the same time she did not want Bali to be killed because he was related to her.

Lord Vishnu was moved by her generosity. He blessed her and said, 'I shall be born as your son to set things right.' But Aditi was worried. How could she bear the great Lord Vishnu in her womb? 'Do not be distressed,' said Lord Vishnu, reading her mind. 'I shall make myself very small.'

Thus Aditi gave birth to a brilliant child, who was Lord Vishnu himself in the form of a dwarf called Vamana.

The Asuras did not want to be left behind. To obtain the blessings of Lord Vishnu, they performed a great yagna to which all were invited. Vamana went there in the guise of a priest to get his share of what was being given away at the yagna. Shukracharya, the guru of the Asuras, recognised him at once and realised that Vishnu had come there on behalf of the gods. Shukracharya warned Bali and told him not to give anything to Vishnu, but Bali would not listen to him. 'There can be no greater fortune than having Vishnu at my yagna,' he said.

He gave a warm welcome to Vamana and got ready to wash his feet with holy water from an urn. Shukracharya used his magical powers to enter the urn and block the spout so that no water could be poured on Lord Vishnu's feet.

Vishnu took a thorn and poked the spout with it. The thorn pierced an eye of Shukracharya. Blinded, and in great agony, Shukracharya fled as fast as he could.

After the yagna, Bali asked Vamana to make a wish. Since he was the ruler of all the three worlds, he thought that he could give Vamana anything he wished for. Vamana made a humble request. All he wanted was three paces of land, measured by his own feet. Bali was happy to grant him his wish.

As soon as his wish was granted, Vamana grew to a gigantic size. His head touched the heavens, and with two enormous steps he covered the entire solar system. 'Where should I place my third step?' he asked Bali. True to his promise, Bali offered his head. Vamana placed his foot on it and pressed it down with tremendous force, sending him to the underworld. Thus Bali became the king of the underworld, and heaven was restored to the gods.

THE PARASHURAMA AVATARA

Once upon a time there lived a king named Gadhi, who had a daughter named Satyavati. Richika was a sage who loved Satyavati. One day he went to Gadhi and asked for her hand in marriage.

Richika was handsome, learned, pious, and full of virtue. But he was extremely poor. He could barely earn enough to have two proper meals a day. The king was not ready to give away his daughter to such a poor man.

As Richika was about to leave, disappointed, Gadhi had second thoughts. 'How can I turn away such a learned man?' he thought to himself. 'People will think ill of me, and Richika will be offended. I must think of a way by which I can put off Richika without actually refusing to grant him his wish.'

So he said to Richika, 'We have a tradition in our family. The groom always gifts something to the bride's family. Will you be able to offer us a gift?' 'If you tell me what gift you desire, I shall certainly try to get it for you,' replied Richika.

Gadhi made a demand for a thousand white horses, each having one black ear. He was sure that Richika would never be able to find a thousand such horses, or pay for them even if he found them. But Richika was able to fulfil his demand with the greatest ease. He did not go to the market to hunt for horses. He didn't even worry about how to get the money. He simply went to Varuna, the god of water, and made his request.

'Go back to your land, O great sage,' said Varuna. 'The horses will appear magically the moment you think of them.'

Filled with joy, Richika went back to his land. As he approached the bank of the Ganges, he thought to himself, 'I wish the horses would come now.' And a thousand horses emerged from the river and the air was filled with the sound of their neighs.

When Richika took the horses to Gadhi, the king was too surprised for words. He could not break his promise now. Satyavati was married to Richika. Richika loved his wife, and Satyavati, too, was very devoted to him. So they lived happily together.

Now, take note of what happened next. Satyavati did not have a child. Her mother, too, had not been blessed with a son. Everyone in the kingdom wished that they could both have sons. Richika prepared two bowls of payas (rice cooked in sweetened milk) – one for his wife and the other for his mother-in-law. When Satyavati was about to give her mother her share of payas, her mother said to her, 'I am your mother and you must obey my wishes. Give me the bowl of payas that Richika has prepared for you.' She said this because she thought that the payas prepared by Richika for his wife would be superior to hers.

Poor Satyavati! What could she do? She could not disobey her mother. So she gave her share of payas to her mother and had her mother's share instead. Through his magical powers Richika got to know what had happened and was not at all happy. 'You should not have done this,' he said to Satyavati. 'Your mother is a queen and you are the wife of a sage. I wanted your son to be a devout Brahmana and his brother to be a valiant Kshatriya. Now that you have exchanged your payas with your mother, your sons have also got exchanged.'

Satyavati was dismayed to hear this. She did not want her son to be a Kshatriya. She begged Richika to find a way out of her trouble. Richika thought for some time and then said, 'All right. Your son will be a Brahmana, but your grandson will have to be a fierce warrior.'

Satyavati's mother gave birth to a son who grew up to be the great sage Vishwamitra, and Satyavati gave birth to a boy who was named Jamadagni. Jamadagni also grew up to be a sage. He married princess Renuka and had five sons. The fifth son was an Avatara of Vishnu. He was named Rama and was destined to be a fierce warrior. He was born to destroy the race of the Kshatriyas, who had grown too powerful and wicked.

When Rama grew up, he went to Mount Gandhamadan and prayed to Lord Shiva. Pleased with his devotion, Lord Shiva gave him wonderful weapons as gifts. One of these weapons was an axe, which could smash massive rocks into tiny pieces. Rama always carried it with him and thus came to be known as Parashurama. 'Parashu' means an 'axe' in Sanskrit.

Parashurama was born in a Brahmana family but had the grim nature of a warrior. One day Jamadagni was angry with his wife for some reason. In a fit of fury, he said to his sons, 'Kill your mother right now!'

None of his other brothers agreed to commit this atrocious crime, but Parashurama obeyed his father's command and chopped off his mother's head! Jamadagni cursed his other sons and turned them into cripples for not having obeyed his orders. To Parashurama he said, 'You obeyed me and performed a very difficult task, my son. You can make any three wishes.'

'If you are pleased with me, please bring back my mother to life and make my brothers normal again,' said Parashurama.

'Don't you want anything for yourself?' asked Jamadagni. 'I want my mother to forget that I killed her. I would also like to be freed from the sin of having killed my mother.' 'So be it,' said his father.

One day when Jamadagni's sons were not present at the hermitage, the mighty king Karthavirya dropped in for a visit. He was the ruler of the Haihaya dynasty. He had been blessed by Sage Dattatraya and endowed with a thousand arms. He rode a golden chariot which could take him wherever he commanded it to. Karthavirya was so fearsome that people trembled at the mere mention of his name.

When Karthavirya came to their ashram, Jamadagni and Renuka served him in the best manner possible, but Karthavirya repaid their hospitality by trampling down the trees of the ashram and stealing a calf of their divine cow Kamadhenu.

Parashurama returned home, and his father told him what had happened. Enraged, Parashurama took his deadly axe and went in search of Karthavirya. Karthavirya was no match for him, even though he had a thousand arms and a thousand weapons. Parashurama chopped him into bits with his axe.

When Karthavirya's sons heard of their father's death, they were furious. They waited for an opportunity to take revenge. One day when Jamadagni's sons were not in the ashram, they came in and killed Jamadagni. Parashurama returned home and found his father's body lying in a pool of blood. The sight filled him with grief, which slowly turned into rage. Soon he grew angrier than anyone has ever been in the entire world.

He performed his father's last rites and lit the funeral pyre. Then he went and killed all the sons and descendants of Karthavirya. But his anger did not subside. He made a vow that he would wipe out the entire race of Kshatriyas! He hunted down all the Kshatriyas of the world and killed them. He did not even spare their children. After he was sure that all the Kshatriyas had died, Parashurama's anger cooled down and he retired into the forest.

A thousand years went by. Some Kshatriya children had survived. They grew up, married, and had children of their own. Thus in a thousand years, there were Kshatriyas again. When Parashurama became aware of this, his anger was roused once more, and the world witnessed another deluge of blood. But after he had killed all the Kshatriyas once again, their widows approached the Brahmanas and requested them to grant them sons. The Brahmanas fathered their children and brought forth a race of valiant Kshatriya boys and girls.

THE RAMACHANDRA AVATARA

In North India, Rama is perhaps the most popular of all the incarnations of Vishnu. Lord Vishnu was born as Rama to destroy Ravana, the ten-headed king of Lanka. The *Ramayana,* the story of Rama, contains some of the most beautiful legends of India that have been told and retold time and again for thousands of years. It is a long story, and an entire book will be needed to give you all the details. What you will be reading here is just an outline of this great epic.

Ayodhya was a beautiful city situated on the banks of the river Sarayu. The people of Ayodhya led a contented life because they were ruled by a wise and just king, Dasaratha. King Dasaratha had three wives—Kaushalya, Sumitra and Kaikeyi; Kaikeyi was his favourite queen. However, none of his wives had a child. Dasaratha was very unhappy because he was getting old and there was no one to succeed him as king.

All the sages in Ayodhya advised Dasaratha to perform a yagna to show his devotion to the gods. Dasaratha followed their advice, and when the yagna was performed, Agni, the god of fire, rose from the flames and presented to the king a bowl of kheer or sweetened milk. The kheer was divided amongst the queens, and in due course all of them gave birth to sons. Kaushalya's son was named Rama, Kaikeyi's son was called Bharata, and Sumitra had twins, who were named Lakshmana and Shatrughna. The whole city of Ayodhya celebrated the birth of the princes. Dasaratha loved all his sons and was especially very proud of Rama, his eldest son who would be king one day.

The four princes grew up and learnt the art of archery, riding, and hunting from Sage Vashishtha. They also learnt the holy scriptures. There was great love amongst the brothers. Lakshmana was Rama's constant companion. Bharata and Shatrughna were inseparable.

When Rama was about sixteen, the great sage Vishwamitra came to Dasaratha's court. He had come to seek Dasaratha's help. He had been trying to perform a yagna but was unable to do so because two Rakshasas, Maricha and Subahu, kept polluting the yagna by pouring human blood and flesh on the fire-pit. Vishwamitra was unable to curse them because he was engaged in holy work.

'These Rakshasas must be killed,' he said to Dasaratha. 'Rama is the only person who can kill them. I would like to take him along with me.'

At first Dasaratha was hesitant to send Rama because he was so young. But Vashishtha told him not to worry. Dasaratha blessed Rama and Lakshmana and sent them with Vishwamitra.

Vishwamitra and the two princes travelled barefoot. On the way, Vishwamitra taught Rama spells and incantations and gave him many powerful weapons. After a long journey, the three of them reached the spot where the yagna was to be performed.

Things went on very smoothly till the last day when all of a sudden blood and pieces of flesh fell into the sacred fire. Rama looked up and saw two demons rushing towards the fire pit. Rama drew out his arrows and killed the demons at once. The holy men were much relieved, and the yagna was successfully completed.

The next day, Vishwamitra and the other sages set out for the city of Mithila. Rama and Lakshmana accompanied them. Mithila was ruled by King Janaka, who was known for his goodness. His beautiful daughter Sita was now of marriageable age. Janaka had just made an announcement that he would get his daughter married to anyone who could string his bow. This was no ordinary bow. It was large and mighty, and had been presented to him by Shiva. Vishwamitra, Rama, and Lakshmana reached Mithila and found that Sita's swayamvara was being held in the wedding hall of the palace. The hall was beautifully decorated and filled with princes and kings who had come there hoping to marry Sita. Ravana, the king of Lanka, was also present. He was confident that he would win Sita's hand.

On Janaka's orders, the mighty bow was brought to the hall. Janaka gave all the princes a chance to string the bow. Many of the princes came forward, but they could not even lift the bow. Ravana fell down while trying to raise it and left the hall in shame. Vishwamitra turned to Rama and urged him to try his strength. Rama took his blessings and walked up to the bow. He lifted the bow effortlessly, and as he was drawing the string, the bow broke into two, to the wonder and fear of all those present.

King Janaka was extremely happy that Rama, the prince of Ayodhya, would wed his daughter. He sent messengers to convey this news to Dasaratha. Dasaratha was delighted to hear the news. He reached Mithila along with his wives, sons, ministers, Vashishtha, and other important people. Rama was married to Sita, and his brothers were married to the three sisters of Sita.

Soon after Rama's wedding, Dasaratha decided to give up his throne and crown Rama as the king. He consulted his ministers and they all thought it was a good idea. Dasaratha immediately made the announcement to the people of Ayodhya, and everyone was delighted.

Kaushalya, Sumitra and Kaikeyi were also happy. But soon, Kaikeyi's maid Manthara poisoned her mind. 'Queen Kaikeyi,' she said. 'You have forgotten that you have a son too. When Rama becomes the king, Kaushalya will treat you like her maid, and Bharata would have to behave like Rama's servant. You are Dasaratha's favourite queen. He should prove it by making Bharata the king.'

Kaikeyi thought Manthara was right. She did not want to be treated like Kaushalya's maid. When Dasaratha came to Kaikeyi's chamber that night, he found that she had torn all her clothes, strewn her jewels all over the floor, and was weeping.

Now, long ago, Dasaratha had granted two wishes to Kaikeyi. When Dasaratha saw her in this state and asked her what was wrong, she reminded him of his wishes. 'I want you to grant the wishes to me now,' she said. Dasaratha agreed and asked her what the wishes were.

Boldly, Kaikeyi said, 'My first wish is that Bharata should be crowned as the king, and the second is that Rama should live as a hermit in the forest. I shall kill myself unless you grant me the wishes right now!'

Dasaratha could not believe what he had just heard. He was shocked by Kaikeyi's mean and selfish demands. He spent the entire night pleading with her and begging her for mercy. But Kaikeyi was relentless. 'You have to keep your word,' she said to him.

The coronation was supposed to take place the next day. The morning dawned. The happy people of Ayodhya were getting ready to attend the coronation ceremony. Vashishtha and the other sages were busy with all the rituals that had to be performed. Dasaratha called Rama and told him about Kaikeyi's desire.

Without any hesitation, Rama said that he was ready to carry out Kaikeyi's wishes. 'I will go and stay in the forest like a hermit if mother wants me to. I shall be very happy to see my brother Bharata as the king. I can even sacrifice my life for him.'

Kaikeyi was delighted when she heard that Rama had acceded to her request. Rama got ready to leave. Kaushalya bade him farewell with a heavy heart. Sita decided to go with her husband. Rama tried to dissuade her, but Sita would not listen. 'Nothing can give me more happiness than being with you,' she said. Lakshmana, too, refused to be left behind.

Rama, Sita and Lakshmana discarded their royal robes and wore coarse saffron clothes. The city of Ayodhya wept when it was time for them to depart. The three of them left Ayodhya and walked barefoot till they reached the forest Dandaka. There they looked for a quiet place and finally settled in the beautiful hills of Chitrakuta.

A short while after Rama's departure, Dasaratha died, pining away for Rama. Ayodhya wept once more. Bharata went to the forest in search of his brothers and Sita. When he met them, he gave them the news of Dasaratha's death. He tried to persuade Rama to return to Ayodhya and rule over it. But Rama refused. 'It is my duty to carry out the wishes of my parents,' he said.

Bharata went back to Ayodhya and placed Rama's sandals on the throne. 'These padukas are your true masters,' he said to the people. 'I am here only as a servant of Rama.' Bharata was a good king, and the people of Ayodhya felt safe and happy under his rule.

Rama, Sita and Lakshmana had many adventures in the forest, where they lived as hermits. They killed many Rakshasas, who used to terrorise the sages in the forest. After ten years of exile, Rama and the others set out for the hermitage of Rishi Agastya, who had magical powers because of the austerities that he performed. There they built a hut, but were not able to live in peace for very long.

One day a demoness named Surpanakha passed by. She saw Rama and Lakshmana talking to each other. Rama's good looks caught her attention and she fell madly in love with him. She went up to him and asked him who he was. After Rama introduced himself, the demoness said, 'I am Surpanakha, the only sister of Ravana. Kumbhakarna, Vibhisana,

Khara, and Dushana are also my brothers. I love you Rama. I have never seen anyone so good-looking. Marry me.'

Rama smiled and replied that he was already married. He asked her to propose to Lakshmana instead. Surpanakha acted on Rama's advice, but Lakshmana sent her back to Rama. Feeling humiliated, she tried to kill Sita, but Rama prevented her from doing so. Lakshmana then chopped off her nose and ears.

Screaming with pain, Surpanakha ran to her brother Khara and told him about how Rama and Lakshmana had humiliated her. 'I want to drink Sita's blood!' she said to him. 'And I want you to behead Rama and Lakshmana,'

Khara was enraged to see his sister in this condition. He took a large army of demons and went in search of Rama. He promised his sister that he would bring back Rama's head. The army of Rakshasas attacked Rama, but he fought them single-handedly, while Lakshmana guarded Sita. Rama destroyed the entire army and killed Khara and Dushana, too.

Surpanakha, who had witnessed the battle and had seen the power of Rama, fled to Lanka. She went to the court of Ravana, crying loudly, and tried to cover her nose where there was now a gaping hole.

Ravana was shocked to see his sister in such a state. Before he could say anything, Surpanakha said, 'Ravana! All the Rakshasas have been killed. Khara and Dushana are dead. And all this has happened due to this one man known as Rama, who is no ordinary man. You should see him when he shoots. It looks as though it is raining arrows.'

When Ravana asked Surpanakha how it all happened, she lied to him. 'Rama had a lovely wife named Sita,' she said to him. 'I wanted to bring her here as a gift for you. Rama got angry and asked Lakshmana to chop off my ears and nose.'

Ravana was very angry when he heard this. To provoke him further, she said, 'Brother, you are strong and mighty. Kidnap Sita and marry her. Our brothers' deaths will be suitably avenged.'

Ravana had attended Sita's swayamvara. He had not forgotten how beautiful she was and how humiliated he had felt when Rama had won her hand. The very next morning, Ravana flew in his Pushpak Viman and reached the home of Maricha, another Rakshasa, and persuaded him to help him kidnap Sita. Maricha turned himself into a golden deer and roamed near Sita's hut. When she came out to pluck flowers, she saw the beautiful creature and was completely charmed by it. She called out to Rama and asked him to catch it for her.

Lakshmana, too, saw the golden deer, but he was a little suspicious. 'I somehow feel that this deer is not a real animal but a Rakshasa in disguise,' he said to Rama. But Rama brushed Lakshmana's fears aside. He told him to look after Sita, while he went to catch the deer.

Rama chased the animal, and as he was about to catch it, the deer picked up speed. Unable to keep up pace, Rama used his bow and arrow. When the arrow pierced the deer, its body turned into that of a Rakshasa. Before he died, Maricha imitated Rama's voice and cried out, 'Sita! Lakshmana!' Rama realised that he had been tricked and hurried back to the ashram.

When Sita heard Rama's cry, she thought that Rama was in danger. She asked Lakshmana to go to his rescue. Lakshmana tried to assure her that no harm could ever come to Rama, but Sita would not listen. She got very angry with Lakshmana and threatened to kill herself if he did not go to help Rama.

Lakshmana was left with no choice. Before he went, he asked Sita to be careful of strangers. He drew a line outside the door of the hut with his arrow. 'Please do not cross this line under any circumstances, dear sister-in-law,' he said to Sita. 'May God protect you.'

As soon as Lakshmana left, Ravana, who was hiding behind a tree, turned himself into a poor Sanyasi and came and begged at Sita's door. Sita brought food and water for him. But she stood at the doorway, not wishing to cross the line that Lakshmana had drawn. Ravana pretended to be very weak with hunger and requested Sita to come up to him with the food.

As soon as Sita crossed the line, Ravana grabbed her hand and revealed his true identity. 'Beautiful Sita!' he said to her. 'I am Ravana, the king of Lanka. I have come to take you with me. I shall make you my queen and provide you with all the luxuries of life.'

Angrily, Sita tried to free herself, but Ravana was much stronger. He dragged her to his Pushpak Viman. Soon they were airborne. Sita called out to Rama and Lakshmana, but there was no response. She spoke to all the trees and birds of the forest and asked them to inform Rama that she was in distress.

Jatayu, the king of birds, heard her cries. He put up a brave fight with Ravana. He scratched and injured his body with his powerful wings and broke Ravana's bow. In his anger, Ravana chopped off his wings and legs. Jatayu fell down.

Sita was very upset because Jatayu had died for her sake. She sat quietly, filled with sorrow, while the Pushpak Viman made its way to Lanka. She looked down and saw a group of monkeys sitting on top of a hill. She took her ornaments, tied them up in a bundle, and threw the bundle down at the monkeys. The monkeys were surprised, but by the time they looked up, the Pushpak Viman had sailed away. Finally, it crossed the sea and reached Lanka.

Ravana kept Sita in his royal palace in Lanka and appointed several Rakshasis to keep an eye on her. They were instructed to treat Sita well. Ravana would visit her every day, carrying expensive gifts for her. And every day he would try to charm her and persuade her to marry him. However, Sita was only disgusted by the way he spoke.

Ravana's patience finally wore off. He gave her a year's time. 'If by then you do not agree to marry me, I shall cut you up into pieces,' he said to her. He ordered the Rakshasis to take Sita to the Ashoka Garden and guard her there.

While all this was happening in Lanka, Rama was almost mad with grief. When he met Lakshmana, after the deer was slain, he knew at once that Sita was in danger. They hurried back to the cottage and were shocked to find it empty. Rama was heartbroken. He wandered about, asking the mountains, rivers and trees to tell him what had happened, but there was no reply.

Rama and Lakshmana kept walking till they found Jatayu, who was badly wounded. 'I am Jatayu,' he said to Rama. 'I fought against Ravana, who has kidnapped Sita.' Rama picked up Jatayu, and Jatayu blessed him and died in his arms.

Rama and Lakshmana went westwards in search of Sita. On their way, they met a Rakshasa named Kabandha, who had arms which were several miles long. As soon as Kabandha saw the princes, he picked them up and was about to swallow them when Rama and Lakshmana chopped off his arms. To their surprise the Rakshasa turned into a handsome youth. Kabandha told them his story. He was once very good-looking, but had the powers to turn himself into a terrifying creature. He would use his power to scare and kill the sages who lived in the forest. He was cursed by one of the sages. 'May you remain hideous till Rama comes to the forest and chops off your arms,' said the sage.

After Kabandha regained his good looks, he commanded his flying machine to take him to heaven. Before leaving, he advised Rama and Lakshmana to take the help of Sugriva, the king of monkeys, who lived in the hills of Rishyamukh by the side of Lake Pampa.

Rama took his advice and left for Rishyamukh. Rishyamukh was a hilly region filled with monkeys. Sugriva was their leader. His commander-in-chief was Hanuman, who was a brave and intelligent monkey. Sugriva was once the king of Kishkinda, but his brother Vali had dethroned him and abducted his wife.

When Rama and Lakshmana reached Rishyamukh, Sugriva thought that Vali had sent them to kill him and was greatly alarmed. He sent Hanuman to find out who they were. Hanuman went and greeted Rama and discovered the purpose of their visit. Thereafter, he carried them on his shoulders and took them to Sugriva.

Sugriva heard Rama's story and promised to help him. Then he suddenly remembered that he had seen a lady being abducted by a Rakshasa. He also remembered that she was crying 'Rama! Lakshmana!' He asked one of the monkeys to fetch the ornaments that Sita had dropped, and asked Rama if they were his wife's. Rama was moved to tears when he saw Sita's jewels. Rama and Sugriva made a pact. Sugriva promised Rama that he would send his Vanara army to rescue Sita. In return, Rama offered to kill Vali and help Sugriva regain his kingdom.

After Rama had fulfilled his promise and Sugriva had got back his kingdom, he asked Hanuman to summon all the monkeys to Kishkinda. Soon thousands of monkeys gathered. They were instructed to hunt for Sita in all possible directions. Rama gave his ring to Hanuman. 'When you see Sita, show her the ring. She will know that I have sent you to her,' he said.

The Vanaras searched for an entire month, but were unable to find her. Tired and defeated, they sat by the seashore discussing what to do next. They dared not go back without any news of Sita. 'I wish we could die like Jatayu, fighting for Sita's sake,' said one of the monkeys.

At the mention of Jatayu's name, a seabird flew up to them and introduced himself as Jatayu's brother Sampati. He told them that he had seen Ravana crossing the sea in his Pushpak Viman with a beautiful lady. He also told them that Ravana lived on the island of Lanka.

The monkeys were happy to know the whereabouts of Sita. But how could they reach Lanka? They would have to cross one hundred leagues of water. Hanuman came to their rescue. He was the son of Vayu and had the speed of wind. He also had the strength to destroy an entire city. He offered to jump across the ocean and land on Lanka.

Then he puffed up his chest and took a deep breath. As he sucked in the air, he grew bigger and bigger in size. Then with a great leap he was airborne. The army of monkeys watched Hanuman with wonder and awe. The gods in heaven showered him with petals. The sun god blessed him by shining less brightly. His father Vayu turned into a gentle breeze and wished him luck.

When Hanuman reached Lanka, he shrunk in size till he was about as small as a cat and managed to slip past the guards and enter the city of Lanka. He searched all over Lanka for a lady of Sita's description, but all he could find were hideous-looking Rakshasis.

Finally he entered the Ashoka Garden and found Sita sitting under a tree. Her clothes were torn and faded. She was surrounded by ugly Rakshasis. Hanuman climbed the tree above her and hid amongst the branches. Soon Ravana appeared and tried his best to woo Sita. But Sita refused to listen to him. 'I am Rama's wife. Rama will surely come to rescue me. And that will be the last day of your life,' she said to him. Ravana ordered the Rakshasis to help Sita change her mind. Then he left and the Rakshasis started pestering Sita. Sita was so overcome with emotion that she decided to hang herself from the tree.

Just then Hanuman called out to her. Taken aback, Sita asked him who he was. Hanuman showed her Rama's ring and told her that he was Rama's messenger. Sita was so happy that tears filled her eyes. She gave one of her ornaments to Hanuman and blessed him. 'Please give my love to Rama and ask him to rescue me soon,' she said.

Hanuman wanted to get some information about Ravana's army. So he trampled and destroyed all the trees in the Ashoka Garden. When the Rakshasas tried to stop him, he killed all of them. Ravana heard about the destruction caused by a single monkey and sent his son Indrajit to capture him.

Indrajit, who was a fearsome warrior, used one of his powerful weapons to capture Hanuman. Hanuman was then dragged to Ravana's court, and he was greatly impressed by the ten-headed Ravana and his grand court.

'Who are you and why have you destroyed the Ashoka Garden?' asked Ravana. Hanuman told him that he was Rama's messenger. He also warned Ravana that he would be destroyed unless he returned Sita to Rama.

Ravana was furious that a monkey dared to talk to him in this manner. He ordered his servants to set Hanuman's tail on fire, and made him walk through the streets of Lanka. When the Rakshasas lit up his tail, Hanuman jumped from building to building and set them on fire. Soon the whole of Lanka was burning! The Ashoka Garden was the only place that Hanuman did not set on fire. He made sure that Sita was safe, and then made his way back to Kishkinda.

Rama was very happy to hear that Sita was unharmed. Sugriva ordered the Vanaras to form an army and march towards Lanka. However, when the army reached the ocean, it had to stop because the monkeys did not know how to cross the vast stretch of water.

Meanwhile, Ravana had quickly rebuilt the city of Lanka. The people of Lanka were afraid of the imminent war. They had seen the havoc caused by one monkey alone. They did not know what would happen when thousands of monkeys descended upon them.

Ravana's younger brother Vibhisana was a devotee of Lord Vishnu. He was courageous enough to tell Ravana that he should send Sita back to Rama before it was too late. Ravana was not pleased with Vibhisana's words and called him a coward.

Vibhisana took four of his supporters and went to Rama to offer him his services. Rama accepted him as a friend and promised to make him the king of Lanka after Ravana was defeated. Vibhisana gave Rama the details of Ravana's army.

Then under the guidance of Vibhisana, the monkeys built a bridge across the ocean by placing logs and sticks. Soon the bridge was ready and the army of monkeys crossed the ocean and attacked Lanka.

A fierce battle took place between the Vanaras and the Rakshasas. The Vanaras fought valiantly and killed many Rakshasas. The Rakshasas also fought well, but it soon became clear that they were losing the war.

Indrajit attacked at night and killed many of them. Then he shot at Rama and Lakshmana with magical arrows that turned into snakes and entwined around the brothers. The poison emitted by the snakes caused Rama and Lakshmana to lose consciousness. Rama quickly recovered, but Lakshmana's body started turning blue. The gods in heaven instructed Garuda, the magical bird of Vishnu, to save Rama and Lakshmana. Garuda swooped down on the serpents and chased them away.

At another point of time, Indrajit hit Lakshmana with a very powerful weapon called Shaktishel. As a result, Lakshmana was unconscious and almost on his death-bed. Hanuman flew to Mount Gandhamadan to fetch a rare herb called Sanjivani. He could not spot the plant. So he transported the entire mountain to Lanka and the prince was saved!

The Vanaras slowly overpowered the army of the Rakshasas. Ravana's brother Kumbhakarna was killed, and so was Indrajit. Soon Rama and Ravana were face to face. Since the two of them were equally powerful, the war continued for days. Finally, Rama used Brahmastra, the mightiest of weapons. It pierced through the armour worn by Ravana and went straight through his heart. The powerful Ravana fell down dead.

The gods in heaven rejoiced, now that the wicked Rakshasa was dead. Rama, the incarnation of Vishnu, had brought back peace on earth. Rama was true to his promise and Vibhisana was crowned the king of Lanka.

Sita was reunited with Rama. Rama, Sita, Lakshmana, Sugriva and Hanuman left for Ayodhya in the Pushpak Viman. When they reached Ayodhya, they found that Bharata was waiting for Rama's return. He begged Rama to take charge of the kingdom. Kaushalya, Kaikeyi, Sumitra and Vashishtha blessed Rama and he became the king.

THE KRISHNA AVATARA

Once upon a time there was a king named Kamsa, who lived in the city of Mathura on the bank of the Yamuna. He was greedy and violent. All his subjects were frightened of him. Mother Earth could not bear the anguish of her people. So she went to Brahma the Creator for help. Brahma felt sorry for her. 'Vishnu is the only one who can help you,' he said. Mother Earth, Shiva, and Brahma then made their way to Lord Vishnu, who dwelt on a snake named Adisesha in an ocean of milk. When they reached the shore of the ocean, they all prayed to Vishnu.

Lord Vishnu was prompt in answering their prayers. He promised that he would be born again on the earth as Krishna to destroy Kamsa.

Kamsa had a beautiful cousin named Devaki. The two of them had grown up together and she was his favourite sister. Kamsa arranged for her marriage with Vasudeva. After the wedding, Kamsa decided to drive them home in his chariot. All of a sudden, he heard a heavenly voice. It said: 'You fool! You are driving Devaki home! Her eighth son is destined to kill you!!'

Kamsa was startled. As soon as he heard the warning, his love for his sister vanished. He dropped the reins, caught hold of her hair, and drew his sword to kill her. Vasudeva came to the rescue of Devaki. He stopped Kamsa and said: 'You are such a great warrior. How can you kill a woman? You are forgetting that she is your favourite sister and today is her wedding day. The voice from heaven said that her eighth child will kill you and not she herself. So please spare her.' To pacify Kamsa, he said that he would hand over every child of Devaki's to him as soon as they were born.

Upon hearing Vasudeva's plea, Kamsa decided not to kill Devaki. However, to protect himself, he imprisoned Vasudeva and Devaki and told the guards to keep a strict watch on them.

Years went by. Vasudeva and Devaki lived in the prison under strict supervision. Vasudeva was true to his promise to Kamsa. He would hand over Devaki's children as soon as they were born, and Kamsa would kill them mercilessly.

Soon it was time for Vishnu to be born on earth. It was late in the night. The sky was clear. Suddenly there was a hushed silence. The stars in the sky began to glow more brightly. The lotus flowers in the lake were in full bloom. There was a gentle breeze. The peacocks began to dance, and all the other birds started to sing. And Devaki gave birth to her eighth son, Krishna.

Vasudeva and Devaki were amazed at the sight of their son because he was very different from other infants. He had four hands in which he held a conch, a chakra, a mace, and a lotus. He had large expressive eyes, and he looked at his parents and smiled in such a manner that all their sorrows vanished. Vasudeva realised at once that this child was divine and had been born to put an end to Kamsa's oppression.

Krishna did not want his parents to remember his divine form. With his powers he turned into an ordinary infant and made his parents forget what they had seen.

Vasudeva and Devaki were now very worried. They knew that Kamsa would not spare this child.

The only way to save him would be to smuggle him out of the prison. But where could they take him? Gokul was a small village on the opposite bank of the Yamuna. Many cowherds dwelt there. Nanda, the head of the village, was Vasudeva's friend. He thought that Krishna would be safe at Nanda's place.

As soon as these thoughts came to Vasudeva's mind, miracles began to occur. The chains that bound Vasudeva's hands and feet came undone. He hid little Krishna in a basket and stealthily walked up to the prison gate. He was surprised to find that all the guards were fast asleep, and the prison gates unlocked themselves.

Vasudeva had to cross the Yamuna in order to reach Gokul. It was raining, and the river was in full spate. Vasudeva carried the basket on his head. Seshanaga, the god of serpents, followed Vasudeva, covering the basket with its hood like an umbrella to protect little Krishna from the rain. The river parted to make way for Vasudeva.

Nanda's wife Yashoda had just given birth to a child. Exhausted after childbirth, she was fast asleep. She did not even know that her child was a girl. Vasudeva placed Krishna next to her and picked up her daughter, who was actually the goddess Durga.

Vasudeva brought her to the prison cell. The door locked itself. It was all very magical. When the guards woke up, they heard the cry of a newborn baby. They immediately went to Kamsa to inform him about the child's birth. Kamsa got up and hurried to the prison cell. It was Devaki's eighth child, the one who was supposed to kill him. Kamsa's hands and feet trembled with nervousness.

When he reached there, Devaki fell at his feet. 'Do not kill my child,' she implored him. 'What can a poor girl do to hurt you? You have already killed so many of my children. Have pity on my daughter.'

But Kamsa was not moved by her words. He snatched the child from Devaki's arms, seized her by her legs, and hurled her against a hard stone slab.But the child, who was actually goddess Durga, slipped from his hands and rose up in the air. She had eight arms, in each of which she held a deadly weapon. The goddess laughed and said, 'You fool! You think that you will be safe by killing me! The child destined to kill you has already been born and is growing up somewhere else. Do not kill innocent children. Search for your real enemy!' Goddess Durga vanished after she said these words.

Kamsa was a devotee of goddess Durga. He was suddenly ashamed of himself for the way he had treated Vasudeva and Devaki. He set them free immediately and begged for their forgiveness. He also decided to hunt all over Mathura for the child who was supposed to kill him.

Krishna grew up in Gokul. Nanda and Yashoda doted on him and showered him with great love. Little Krishna was a bright, mischievous, and adorable child. Every day he would do something naughty that would amuse and charm all his neighbours. The milkmaids of Gokul loved to play with him. They would use colourful flowers and peacock feathers to make ornaments for little Krishna.

Meanwhile, Kamsa had not forgotten the prophecy. His spies, who had been hunting for Krishna all over the kingdom, finally found that the child they were looking for was growing up in Nanda's house in Gokul. When Kamsa heard this, he immediately thought of a plan to kill the child. He called a Rakshasi named Putana.

Putana was very frightening. She was as dark as the night. Her eyes were like two fireballs. Her nose was like a mountain, with nostrils like two caves. Her hands were like pillars, and her legs as thick as tree trunks. Her flaming red hair made her look all the more frightful. She could fly wherever she desired and could assume any form. She also loved to eat young children!

Putana was as cunning and wicked as Kamsa himself. She bared her horrible teeth and grinned gleefully when she heard Kamsa's plan. She assured him that his plan would be carried out successfully, and then flew off.

Putana turned into a beautiful young woman and reached Gokul. Dressed in a splendid saree, and adorned with jewels, she looked very attractive. The people of Gokul were charmed. The milkmaids or gopis thought that she was a goddess. No one could have imagined that she was a wicked Rakshasi who wanted to kill little Krishna.

Putana found her way to Nanda's house. Yashoda saw her and thought that she was a gopi who had come to play with Krishna. Putana found Krishna lying on his cot. She told Yashoda that she would look after Krishna while Yashoda completed her household chores.

Putana picked up Krishna and placed him on her lap. Then she hummed a tune to win his confidence.

Her plan was to poison Krishna. She offered him her breast, which had poisoned milk.

As Krishna sucked the milk, he also started sucking out her life. Putana screamed in agony and begged Krishna to stop sucking. But Krishna would not listen. The earth trembled at the sound of Putana's screams. Before she died, she regained her original form. Yashoda and the others rushed to the courtyard. They were amazed to find the hideous Rakshasi lying dead on the floor and Krishna sitting on top of her.

The people of Gokul realised that Krishna was no ordinary child.

Krishna and Balarama grew up in Nanda's house. Balarama was the son of Rohini, who was Vasudeva's first wife. Both the children were very naughty and their exploits brought cheer to the lives of the villagers of Gokul. The brothers looked very different from each other. Balarama was plump and fair, while Krishna was dark. Krishna would often ask his mother why he was dark and his mother would smile at his innocence. Both the brothers wore anklets, which tinkled as they moved and made it easier for Rohini and Yashoda to keep an eye on them.

One of their favourite pastimes was to tug at the tails of calves. The calves would get annoyed and start running, dragging the children behind them. Krishna and Balarama would return home covered with mud, to the exasperation of their mothers.

Krishna was known as the 'makhanchor' or the 'butter thief' of Gokul. He would lead his friends into the room where gopis kept their butter and curd. The butter was always kept in a pot which hung from the ceiling, well out of Krishna's reach. Stealing butter from the pot was a challenge for Krishna. He would make his friends form a tower by climbing on one another's shoulders. Krishna would climb to the top of the tower and steal the butter. At times when they were caught red-handed, Krishna would smile innocently and ask the gopis why he would steal butter when there was so much butter in his own house!

There are many stories about Krishna's child-hood. One day Balarama and his friends came running to Yashoda. 'Krishna is eating mud,' they said to her. Yashoda was very angry. She went looking for Krishna and found him sitting in the corner of the garden, eating mud with great relish. Yashoda pulled him up and said, 'What are you doing? How can you possibly eat mud?'

'I am not eating mud,' said Krishna. 'You can look into my mouth and see for yourself,' and he opened his mouth wide so that his mother could peer inside. Yashoda looked into his mouth and was amazed by what she saw. Inside little Krishna's mouth was the entire universe! She could see all the stars, constellations, the Milky Way, the sun, the moon, all the oceans, mountains, forests, rivers, and lakes. Yashoda closed her eyes. She did not know what to do. With Krishna around, miracles were a regular feature in her life.

Kamsa had sent many Rakshasas to live near Gokul. They would kidnap people and kill them for no rhyme or reason. The villagers lived in constant fear because they did not know who the next victim would be.

One day all the villagers gathered to find a solution. The wise men had different suggestions to make, but the best solution offered was that they should vacate Gokul and dwell in the forests of Vrindavan. Vrindavan's pastures would be ideal for their cattle.

The villagers, along with their cattle and other belongings, moved to Vrindavan. When they reached there, they were charmed by its greenery. The men got busy building houses and cow sheds. The women had to make arrangements for food. Krishna, Balarama, and the other boys were given the responsibility of grazing the cattle.

The boys would take the cows to the pastures and spend their time playing while they grazed. At times Krishna would play a tune on his flute and the boys would be enchanted by the music. Sometimes they would dance and their anklets would tinkle together. One of their favourite pastimes was to imitate the sounds of animals and birds. Their lives were filled with peace and joy once more.

One day Krishna and his friends took a different route and reached another spot further down the Yamuna. They did not know how dangerous the place was. It was the home of Kaliya the snake, who dwelt in the river with his family. Kaliya had a hundred and one hoods. He was so full of venom that the water in that area had turned poisonous. All the trees and grass by the riverside were wilting. Even the birds that flew over the river would drop down dead. Kaliya was very proud of his poisonous self.

It was a hot day and the boys were thirsty. They went down to the river to drink water without realising that the water was poisoned. As soon as they took a gulp of water, their heads started reeling and they lost consciousness. Krishna understood at once what had happened. He decided to teach the snake a lesson. He climbed up a tree by the river and, with a great leap, dived into the water.

The water in the river splashed in all possible directions. Kaliya was used to a tranquil life. 'Who has dared to invade my territory?' he cried. He raised his hundred and one hoods from the water and was surprised to see a small boy smiling at him. 'Is he a fool?' thought Kaliya. 'How could he have come here without my permission? I am not going to let him escape alive.' Then to punish Krishna, he entwined himself around the boy.

The other boys, who were watching from the bank of the river, were terrified. Some of them ran back to inform Yashoda. All the villagers came running to the spot. Yashoda was trembling with fright and was unable to speak. She wanted to jump into the water to save Krishna. Balarama held her back. 'Believe me, no one can harm Krishna,' he said to her.

Krishna started growing in size. Soon he became so big that Kaliya could not hold him in his grasp. He had to let go of him.

Kaliya was now very angry. He attacked Krishna by spreading his hoods and blowing poison through his nostrils. Krishna started moving very swiftly in the water. The dreaded Kaliya chased him with his hoods raised and his fangs poised to strike. Just when the serpent was sure that he had got Krishna, the boy would slip out of his grasp and the game would continue. Soon the snake got frustrated. It was too tired to chase the boy. Krishna leaped into the air and landed on one of its hoods. Then he started playing his flute and dancing to the music. He would jump from one hood to another, while he performed his dance. The snake was now badly injured and started vomiting blood.

Kaliya's wives pleaded with Krishna and begged him to spare Kaliya's life. Krishna took pity. He did not kill the snake on the condition that the snake would move out of the river and return to the sea.

The water of the Yamuna became pure and sweet again. The trees and grass by the riverside began to flourish once more.

There is another story about Krishna and Mount Govardhan. One day Krishna saw that all the villagers were getting ready to perform some Puja. He asked his father what the matter was. His father told him that the villagers would pray to Lord Indra, the god of rain and thunder. 'It is very necessary to please Lord Indra', explained Nanda. 'The clouds are his representatives and they provide us with water, which is essential for life. We pray to Indra every year so that we get sufficient rain.'

Krishna disagreed. He said, 'Father, haven't we learnt that one reaps as one sows. If we work hard and do good deeds, why should we have to please the gods so that they reward us?'

Nanda and the other villagers argued with Krishna. 'We can't hope for good luck unless the gods are satisfied with us,' they said. The gods are whimsical beings. If they get angry, we may not get any rain at all. And without rain, there will be no fodder for the cattle, no milk for us, and no water for the fields. We cannot afford to displease the gods.'

Krishna tried to reassure the villagers. He said that god was kind and that he looked after those who did their work with honesty and sincerity. 'We should pray to Mount Govardhan instead,' said he. 'After all, we are dependent on its pastures for our livelihood.'

The villagers were now convinced. They made all the arrangements for the Puja. Priests were called and everyone started praying to Mount Govardhan.

When Indra saw that they were praying to a mountain instead of worshipping him, he was furious. Was a mere mountain more important than him, the god of thunder and rain? He decided to punish the villagers. He summoned all the clouds and told them to gather over Vrindavan and rain with all their might.

All of a sudden the skies of Vrindavan were overcast with clouds, and it started to rain. Along with the rain came deadly storms. Soon all the houses were flooded with water, and there was much confusion everywhere.

The people of Vrindavan approached Krishna and asked him what they should do. 'You are very powerful. You have protected us from so many demons. Please save us from Indra's wrath. Should we pray to him for mercy?'

Krishna asked the villagers to follow him. He led them to Mount Govardhan. Then he lifted the entire mountain on his little finger with great ease and asked the people to stand beneath the mountain for shelter.

Slowly the people gathered their flocks and stood beneath Govardhan. The mountain was an umbrella that protected them from the torrential downpour. It rained continuously for seven days, and for seven days Krishna balanced the mountain on his little finger without getting tired.

Indra was astonished by Krishna's feat. When he realised that he would not be able to do anything to the villagers, he withdrew the clouds. It stopped raining. The villagers emerged from beneath the mountain and Krishna gently put it back in its original place.

Krishna saved the people of Gokul from the Rakshasas sent by Kamsa many a time. Kamsa was now getting frustrated.

One day, while Kamsa was lost in thought, Narada, the divine sage, paid him a visit. He told Kamsa that his suspicions were correct and that Krishna was the eighth child of Devaki, the one who was supposed to kill him. Narada advised Kamsa to invite Krishna to Mathura and get him killed.

Accordingly, Kamsa thought of a plan. He called Akrura, one of the renowned citizens of Mathura, to his palace and explained him how he would get Krishna killed. 'You will invite Krishna and Balarama to a wrestling tournament in Mathura,' he said to him. 'Kuvalyapida the elephant will be posted at the main gate. Kuvalyapida has the strength of a hundred elephants. Trampling Krishna and Balarama to death will be an easy task for him. And if they somehow manage to escape from the elephant, my wrestlers will surely kill them during the tournament. If my plan succeeds, no one will blame me, and my enemies will be dead.'

Akrura went to Vrindavan to invite Krishna and Balarama to the wrestling match. Now, Akrura was an ardent admirer of Krishna. After inviting them to Mathura, he told Krishna and Balarama what Kamsa's actual plan was. He begged them not to come to Mathura. But Krishna smiled and said, 'Do not worry for our safety. We shall surely go to Mathura and accept Kamsa's challenge. Kamsa will not be successful in his attempt to kill us. If we don't go to Mathura, people will think that we are cowards.'

Krishna and Balarama took permission from Nanda, Yashoda and Rohini, and set off. At Mathura, they were stopped by the gigantic elephant Kuvalyapida, who stood at the main gate. The elephant charged at them. Krishna caught the elephant's trunk and whirled him round and round till the elephant was quite dizzy. When the elephant tried to attack Krishna again, Krishna pulled out his tusk. Kuvalyapida fell on the ground and moaned in agony.

Kamsa was shocked to hear that Krishna had lifted Kuvalyapida and flung him aside like a toy. However, he was sure that his wrestlers would be able to overpower Krishna.

The courtyard where the wrestling tournament was to be held was beautifully decorated with flowers. All the cowherds of Vrindavan and the citizens of Mathura were seated there, waiting for the matches to begin.

Kamsa's wrestlers—Chanura, Mushtik, Kuta, Shala and Toshala came to the wrestling ground, twirling their moustaches. Krishna and Balarama were called to fight them. The wrestlers were far bigger and stronger than the two boys. Many of the spectators objected because it would be an unequal match. But Kamsa paid no heed.

Chanura was chosen to wrestle with Krishna, and Mushtik had to fight Balarama. The match began. Krishna and Balarama used all the tactics of wrestling and slowly overpowered Chanura and Mushtik.

When Chanura and Mushtik fell down, other wrestlers came to take their place. The brothers defeated Kuta, Shala and Toshala, too. When the remaining wrestlers saw what had happened, they fled as fast as they could.

The spectators were overjoyed to see the two boys winning the tournament. They blew trumpets and clapped. Even the people of Mathura cheered for Krishna and Balarama because they hated the cruel king Kamsa.

But what about Kamsa? He was enraged by the victory of the brothers. He told his men to throw Krishna and Balarama out of Mathura. He gave his soldiers orders to kill Vasudeva. He also asked the guards to imprison his own father Ugrasena, who had supported his enemies.

When Krishna heard about Kamsa's orders, he charged towards him. Kamsa drew his sword to kill Krishna, but Krishna caught his hand and dragged him to the courtyard. First Kamsa's crown fell. Then Kamsa fell to the ground. Krishna climbed on to his chest and hit him hard. That was the end of the cruel king of Mathura.

The people of Mathura rejoiced. They were immensely grateful to Krishna. Krishna and Balarama went to the prison and freed their parents. Ugrasena was made the ruler of Mathura once more. Peace and prosperity returned to Mathura and Mother Earth was contented.

THE BALARAMA AVATARA

Krishna's brother Balarama was also an Avatara of Vishnu. Some people believe that Buddha, and not Balarama, was the ninth Avatara, but there is much controversy about Buddha's role as an incarnation of Vishnu. That is why I have not included the life of Buddha in this book.

Krishna was produced from a black, and Balarama from a white, hair of Vishnu. As the two brothers were constant companions during their stay on earth, most of their adventures are also common. However, there are some stories with Balarama as the central character. Here are a few of them:

A year before his birth, Vishnu transferred Balarama from Devaki's womb to Rohini's, who was another wife of Vasudeva, to save him from Kamsa's wrath. And when Balarama was a year old, he was brought to Nanda's and Yashoda's house so that the two brothers could grow up together.

Balarama, too, possessed miraculous powers. One day while Balarama was playing with the other cowherds in the forest, they asked him to shake some fruit trees belonging to a demon named Dhenuka, so that they might enjoy the fruits. Balarama started shaking the fruit trees. Just then Dhenuka appeared in the form of a monster. When he tried to kick Balarama, the boy seized him by his hind legs, swung him around, and threw him to the ground with such force that the demon died instantly. Balarama flung his dead body to the top of a palm tree. When the demon's friends came to avenge his death, Balarama killed them all.

After Dhenuka's death, the orchard became a favourite spot of the cowherds. One day a demon named Pralamba came to the orchard in the guise of a boy and joined them in their games. He persuaded Balarama to climb onto his shoulders and then ran off with him. When Balarama realised what had happened, he decided to punish the demon by growing heavier. As he grew heavier and heavier, the demon also increased his bulk, until he was as vast as a mountain! Balarama trembled with fear and chanted Krishna's name for help. Krishna reminded him of his divine nature. 'Remember who you are and destroy the demon yourself,' said he. Balarama acted upon his advice. He squeezed the demon with his knees and pummeled him so fiercely with his fists that the demon fell down dead.

When Balarama grew up to be a man, he would always carry his plough with him. Once when he was drunk, he ordered the river Yamuna to come to him so that he might bathe in her. When Yamuna refused, he threw his plough into the stream, dragged her towards him, and made her follow him wherever he went! Finally his anger subsided and he set her free.

The story of his marriage is also interesting. King Raivata had a daughter named Revati. The king wanted a suitable husband for his daughter. So he went to heaven to ask Brahma for his advice. Brahma detained him in heaven for ages, describing the virtues of Vishnu. When Raivata finally returned to the earth, he was surprised to find that during his long absence, men had deteriorated in size, goodness, and strength. However, he followed Brahma's advice, went to Dwaraka, and offered his daughter to Balarama, who accepted his offer. Balarama was astonished at his bride's enormous height. However, with the help of his plough, he was able to reduce her to a suitable size!

The two brothers—Krishna and Balarama—were the best of friends. Only once there was a terrible quarrel between them. This is what happened:

They suspected that a man named Satadhanwan had stolen a precious gem. Krishna and Balarama followed him and reached a part of the country where the roads were very bad. The horses could not pull the chariots through the roads. Balarama stayed back with the chariot and Krishna followed the supposed thief on foot. He beheaded the man with his chakra, but could find no gem.

When Krishna returned empty-handed, Balarama thought that Krishna had stolen the gem. He flew into a rage. 'Shame on you for being so greedy!' said Balarama. 'You are no brother of mine. Our paths are now different. I shall not go back to Dwaraka with you.' And then he proceeded to Videha, where he stayed as a guest of King Janaka for three years till his anger finally cooled down. He realised that he had misjudged his brother and returned to Dwaraka.

Balarama was a neutral observer when the battle of Mahabharata was fought. He died around the same time as Krishna.

THE KALKI AVATARA

The Kalki Avatara, according to Indian mythology, is yet to be born. He is the hope of the Hindus, who believe that Vishnu will be born again on earth as Kalki, to restore peace and prosperity.

According to the Puranas, we are now in the Kali Yuga, when dishonesty and evil will be stronger forces than goodness. In due course of time, a king named Vishwasphatika, the ruler of Magadha, will wipe out the entire Kshatriya race. Barbarians and outcasts will come to power in North India. These kings will be cruel and violent. They will kill women and children at random. They will seize the property of their subjects, and their greed will be insatiable. Piety will slowly decrease. People will devote themselves solely to making money. No spot on earth will be considered holy, and the people will value the earth only for its minerals. Dishonesty will be the order of the day.

Common men will be so tormented by their rulers that they will take refuge in the valleys. They will gladly feed on wild honey, herbs, roots, and fruits. They will use the bark of trees to cover themselves. People will not live beyond the age of twenty-three, and the human race will approach extinction.

At the end of the Kali Yuga, when the people will have forgotten all the practices taught by the Vedas, a divine being shall descend on earth. He will be born in the family of a renowned Brahmana of Sambhal village. He will be known as Kalki and endowed with eight supernatural strengths. He will use his irresistible might to destroy all the wicked rulers and all those whose minds are devoted to injustice and sin. He will then re-establish justice on earth. The minds of those who live at the end of the Kali Yuga will be awakened and made as clear as crystal. And the world will enter the Krita Age or the Age of Purity.

Kalki is depicted as a white man riding upon or bowing down before a white horse. He carries a sword in his hand and is the restorer of goodness and purity.

TALES FROM THE *MAHABHARATA*

THE STORY OF CREATION AND DOOMSDAY

It is written in the *Mahabharata* that there was complete darkness before Creation took place. The first thing to be created was an egg. Each and everything in the universe had its seed within the egg.

When this egg hatched, Lord Brahma came out first. Then slowly all the gods and goddesses, demons and Rakshasas appeared. After that the earth, water, and the wind were formed.

Lord Brahma had several sons. Seven of them—Marichi, Atri, Angiraha, Pulasta, Pulaha, Kratu and Vashishta—are known as the Saptarshis or the seven wise men. From Brahma's heart, Dharma and Bhrigu were born. Daksha was created from his big toe. Daksha had fifty daughters. Marichi's son Kashyap married thirteen of them. These daughters are the mothers of all the gods, goddesses, Gandharvas and Apsaras.

However, all the creatures of the earth have not descended from them. Rakshasas, monkeys, and apes are the descendants of Pulasta. Lions, tigers, and other animals can be traced back to Pulah. Other creatures have other ancestors.

The universe is very old today, and when Doomsday arrives, everything that came into existence will be destroyed. And then it will be time for Creation to start all over again. Just as day is followed by night and night is once again followed by day, in exactly the same manner, Creation is followed by destruction and then by Creation again. It is as if the universe is a grand web which our Creator folds and unfolds continuously.

What are the four stages of a man's life? They are childhood, youth, middle age, and old age. According to our ancient scripts, the life of the universe can also be divided into four stages – the Satyuga, the Tretayuga, the Dvaparyuga, and the Kaliyuga.

In the Satyuga, everyone was good and tall. It is said that men were twenty one feet high! In the

Tretayuga, there appeared some evil in the world and men grew shorter. But they were still fourteen feet in height. In the Dvaparyuga, men were only seven feet tall, and there were equal amounts of good and evil on the earth. Now we are all in the Kaliyuga. People are even shorter today. While doing one good deed, they end up doing three evil ones! And when the world finally becomes completely evil, and as useless as a dirty, torn, old piece of cloth, our Creator will destroy it and it will be the Judgment Day. This is an eternal cycle.

On Doomsday, all those who are immortal also meet their end, the only exception being Markandeya Rishi, who never dies. The Pandavas met this extraordinary man during their exile in the forest. At that time he had told Yudhishthira that he had seen Doomsday and that he would continue to live even after another Day of Judgment. No one knows how many thousands of years old Markandeya Rishi is. But looking at him you will never be able to guess his age because he looks about twenty-five!

Although he hadn't died during Doomsday, Markandeya Rishi had been greatly inconvenienced and had also seen many strange sights at that time.

Long before Doomsday, the earth became very dry and the rains never came. All the plants and trees perished. Small animals died of starvation. Then one day seven suns rose in the sky. In the heat of the suns, the rivers, lakes, seas, and oceans dried up. All the grass, trees, and wood got scorched and turned into ashes. After that a dreadful fire lit up and caused mayhem everywhere. It reached right up to hell, and the gods, demons, and Rakshasas were all equally agitated by it. Slowly all the living things on the planet died in this fire.

Then the clouds appeared—red clouds, yellow ones, blue ones, black ones, clouds as big as elephants, clouds as huge as mountains. With flashes of lightning and the sound of thunder, the rains poured from the skies and created havoc in heaven and hell. It rained so much that the great fire was put out. The rains flooded the earth completely and submerged all the mountains. It poured continuously for twelve whole years. By the time it stopped raining, everything in the universe got immersed in water.

No one knows how Markandeya Rishi survived all this. However, being ravenously hungry, getting scorched by the fire, and floating in water for twelve long years must have been extremely agitating for him. Luckily for him, in the midst of all this destruction, he spotted a gigantic Banyan tree. When he went closer, he found that there was a wonderfully comfortable bed on its branches. And sitting on the bed was a blue-skinned boy as beautiful as a full moon night.

Although Markandeya Rishi had seen fantastic sights, he was surprised to see the boy. How could the boy have survived all the terrible destruction? he wondered. Although Markandeya Rishi was omniscient, that is, he knew everything about the

past, present and the future, he could not understand how this miracle had occurred.

The boy, however, was not surprised to see Markandeya Rishi. As soon as he saw him, he said, 'You must be very tired, Markandeya. Come, rest inside my tummy.' Saying this, he opened his mouth and Markandeya went through it into the boy's stomach!

Another surprise awaited him there. Instead of being digested, he found that he was back in his own universe and was free to move about as he pleased! The old world was intact with the same Himalayas, the Ganges, all the villages, towns, and holy places. The people, the markets, and all the delights that the world had to offer were there!

For thousands of years, Markandeya Rishi dwelled inside the stomach of this strange and beautiful boy, but couldn't find a way out. He thought that the boy was someone very special and started reflecting on him. As soon as he started praying, he found that he had come out of the boy's tummy and that the boy was peacefully sitting on the bed on top of the branches of the Banyan tree. 'Are you well rested?' asked the boy.

It was then that Markandeya realised that the boy was none other than Lord Vishnu himself. 'Brahma is asleep now,' said Lord Vishnu. 'When he wakes up, Creation will start all over again. Meanwhile, you can rest here.'

Saying this, Lord Vishnu vanished into thin air. The process of Creation started all over again. This is what the *Mahabharata* says about Creation and Doomsday.

THE STORY OF CHYAVAN AND SUKANYA

Maharishi Chyavan was the son of Bhrigu. The tale of his meditation is quite extraordinary. He sat by a lake in the forest and meditated. No one can say how long his penance lasted, but slowly his body got covered with dust, which turned into mud. Plants grew out of the mud, and ants built nests on these plants. However, Chyavan continued with his penance. Finally, he looked like a termite hill, which the people in that area began to revere. They had heard from their great grandfathers that Maharishi Chyavan was meditating inside the termite hill.

One day, many years later, a king named Sharjati brought his family and friends for a picnic in the forest. There were many little girls in the group who had never been to a forest. 'What tree is that?'; 'What flower is this?'; 'Is this fruit edible?' were some of the questions they pestered the grown ups with.

The king had a daughter named Sukanya, who was very intelligent and extremely beautiful. As she was an only child, her parents doted on her; and as a result she was whimsical in many ways.

The princess, along with her friends, walked through the forest and reached the termite hill. Chyavan had just completed his meditation. He opened his eyes and saw the princess, whose face glowed with beauty and innocence.

Chyavan's heart was filled with affection for Sukanya. He wanted to be introduced to her so that he could say a few nice things to her. But since he hadn't eaten for ages, his throat was parched and he couldn't utter a single word.

Sukayna was amazed at the sight of the termite hill. She had never seen anything like that before. When she came closer to inspect the hill, she noticed two small objects sparkling like gems. The princess had a stick in her hand, which she had picked up from somewhere. She poked the small objects with the stick, out of curiosity. The sparkling objects were nothing but Maharishi Chyavan's eyes, which were now open. You can imagine how badly hurt he must have been when Sukanya poked his eyes with the stick. He didn't leap into the air because he was covered with so much mud, and he didn't cry out aloud because his throat was parched and dry.

But he was FURIOUS. In his anger, he cursed the king's men so that a strange disease, which affected their brains and made them go round the bend with fear and confusion, infected them.

The king was extremely surprised and worried to see his men behaving in that fashion. Then a thought struck him. 'I hope you haven't shown any disrespect to the sage who dwells within the termite hill,' he said to his men. 'We haven't been anywhere near the hill,' replied his men. 'Maybe we can ask the sage why this has happened to us.'

Sukanya overheard the conversation between her father and his men. She understood what had happened and quickly confessed to her father what she had done. The king ran to the termite hill and apologised to the sage. 'My daughter has caused you a lot of pain,' he said. 'Please forgive her. She did it unknowingly.'

Then Chyavan said something quite astonishing. 'I will forgive your beautiful, eccentric daughter only if you get me married to her!' he said. The king was thunderstruck! Here was a man at least a thousand years old, who hadn't eaten anything for so long that he was just a bag of bones, and he wanted to marry his precious daughter! The king did not know what to do.

He had very little choice. His men were going quite mad because of the sage's curse. And the sage would not lift the curse unless the king got his daughter married to him. The king was forced to agree to Chyavan's demand.

But he was not at all happy. In fact, the entire kingdom mourned at the poor girl's fate. However, the strange thing was that Sukanya did not seem to be unhappy at all. 'I gave him such pain and yet this saintly man has so much affection for me that he wishes to marry me!' thought Sukanya. 'It is my duty to serve this man and look after his needs.'

The pundits found a suitable date, and arrangements were made for the wedding. The wedding took place, but no one rejoiced—no one except Sukanya. After the wedding, Sukanya dressed as an ascetic and went to live in the forest with her husband. There she led a contented life, looking after her husband's needs and thinking about god.

One day the Ashwini brothers (who are the divine doctors) spotted Sukanya standing near her cottage. They were taken aback by the sight of her, and wondered what such a beautiful woman was doing in the forest. They stopped by and asked her who she was. 'I am King Sharjati's daughter and Chyavan Rishi's wife,' replied Sukanya.

The Ashwini twins were amused by her reply. 'How could your father get you married to this old man?' they said. 'This man can't even feed you or clothe you properly. Look at your tattered clothes! You are so beautiful. You should be adorned with diamonds and pearls. Marry one of us and you shall stay in comfort in heaven.'

Sukanya was angered by the twins' remarks. 'I love my husband and am totally devoted to him,' she replied irritably. 'Do not insult him in front of me.' Her rebuke had no effect on the twins. They had magical powers and decided to use these to trick her into marrying one of them. 'We wish to transform your husband into a handsome young man. Go and ask him if he has any objections,' said they.

Sukanya went and asked Chyavan and he agreed. 'Tell me what I have to do,' said he. 'All you have to do is to take a dip in this pond,' said the twins.

As Chyavan got into the pond to take a dip, the two naughty gods hid inside the pond. And when Chyavan emerged from the water, so did the twins, and now the three of them looked identical!

The Ashwini twins had thought that they would confuse Sukanya by transforming Chyavan and making him look like them. But fooling an intelligent woman like Sukanya was not such an easy task. Sukanya noticed that although the three of them looked identical, there was a difference in their facial expressions. She could not mistake the affection with which Chyavan gazed at her. Happily she went up to him and stood next to him.

The unfortunate part was that Chyavan was kind and forgiving. If he had been as bad-tempered as Durvasa Rishi, the meddlesome gods would have got their just rewards there and then. But Chyavan Rishi was too good-natured. He said, 'I was old and feeble. You made me young and handsome again. The gods drink somrasa (a sort of wine made from the juice of a plant), without offering you any. I will see to it that you get your share.'

The Aswini twins went away, pleased with the way things had turned out. The news that Chyavan had turned into a handsome youth quickly reached Sharjati. He was so delighted with the news that he took his men and arrived at Chyavan Rishi's ashram. They all lived there for a few happy years. Then one day Chyavan said to Sharjati, 'I wish to perform a yagna for your sake. Please make the necessary arrangements.'

The arrangements were made and Chyavan started performing the yagna. All the gods were present at the yagna. There were many earthen pots containing somrasa for them. Chyavan started distributing the somrasa amongst the gods. He set aside two bowls for the Ashwini twins. Indra objected. 'The Ashwini twins are minor gods. They are just our doctors. They cannot be given a share of the wine. Chyavan disobeyed Indra and started to pour wine for the twins. Indra was furious and threatened to strike him with a thunderbolt.

Chyavan paid no attention to his warning and continued with his task. Indra produced a thunderbolt and aimed it at Chyavan. All the gods trembled with fear, but Chyavan was not afraid. He chanted a few mantras and poured some ghee into the fire. And out of the fire came a terrible Asura, more ferocious than anything on earth. When the Asura opened his mouth, his lower lip touched the ground and his upper lip reached the skies.

Everyone could see that his teeth were hundreds of yards long. His eyes burnt like the sun. He was so huge that no one could see his hands or legs. When this monstrous creature took out his tongue and licked his lips, everyone thought that he would swallow the entire Creation! The creature looked at Indra and grunted in a horrible manner. 'Save me!' shouted Indra, 'Please give somrasa to the Ashwini twins.'

So that is how the twins became entitled to a share of the wine. Chyavan had fulfilled his promise. He went back to the ashram with Sukanya and led a peaceful life.

THE STORY OF SATYAVAN AND SAVITRI

King Ashwapati was the ruler of a kingdom named Madra. He was wise and just. All his subjects were happy under his rule. However, the king was sad because he did not have a child of his own.

For eighteen years the king prayed to goddess Savitri for a child. Pleased with his devotion, the goddess rose from the fire at the end of eighteen years. 'You can make a wish and I shall grant it,' she said.

The king fell at her feet and said that he wanted many children. 'I have already spoken to Brahma,' said the goddess. 'And you will be blessed with a daughter of great beauty and virtue.'

Soon the queen gave birth to a daughter as beautiful as the moon. She was named Savitri after the goddess who had blessed the king. All the people in the kingdom were amazed by Savitri's beauty. She looked as though she had been made by mixing gold with the early morning sunlight. As Savitri grew up, her thoughts turned towards god. She looked so bright and intelligent that princes were scared of her. No one had the courage to ask for her hand in marriage!

The king was unhappy because there were no suitors for his daughter. One day he said to her, 'I will give you a golden chariot. Take some people with you and go around the country. If you find a prince whom you like, I shall get him married to you.' Savitri blushed when her father said these words.

The king's old minister made arrangements for Savitri's journey. He chose travelling companions for her. He also decorated a golden chariot for her and brought it to her doorstep. The princess took her parents' blessings and set off. They went to many holy places, visited many shrines. The princess gave away many things as charity and was very happy throughout the journey.

When Savitri returned home after a long time, Ashwapati was engaged in conversation with

Narada, the divine sage. When Narada saw Savitri, he asked her father, 'Where had your daughter gone? I can see that she is quite grown up. Why isn't she married?' Ashwapati explained to him that he had sent his daughter on a tour of the kingdom so that she could choose a husband.

The king turned to his daughter and asked her if she had met the right prince. Savitri did not want to answer her father because Narada was sitting right there. However, she was an obedient daughter. In an embarrassed manner, she replied, 'I have chosen Satyavan, the son of Dyumatsena, as my husband.'

Now, Dyumatsena was the king of Salva. He had been driven out of his kingdom by his enemies, after he went blind. The king and the queen had taken refuge in the forest with their little son Satyavan, who was now a young man.

Narada got a shock when he heard Savitri's answer. He shook his head and said, 'You have done something very wrong, my dear.' The king asked him to explain what he meant. 'Satyavan is a wonderful young man,' replied Narada. 'He is as bright as the sun, as good-looking as the Ashwini twins, and as intelligent as Brihaspati. You will not find another man who is as simple, truthful and pious as Satyavan.'

'Then what is wrong with him?' asked the king, in a worried manner. Narada replied, 'Satyavan is destined to die in a year from today. This one fact eclipses all of Satyavan's virtues.'

With great sadness, the king turned to his daughter and said, 'Please don't marry him, my child.' 'In my heart I have already accepted him as my husband. It does not matter if he is going to die in a year's time. I will not change my decision,' said Savitri.

Narada was moved by Savitri's words. He said, 'I admire your daughter's strength of purpose and firmness of mind. Please get her married to Satyavan. You will not find a more virtuous man.'

'You are my divine teacher,' said the king. 'I accept your advice.' Narada blessed them and left. Ashwapati started making preparations for Savitri's wedding. He fixed a date for the occasion. Then along with the Brahmanas, pundits and his daughter, he went to the forest where Dyumatsena stayed. Dyumatsena welcomed the king and asked him the purpose of his visit.

'I have come here with a request. My daughter Savitri is very beautiful and talented. Please accept her as your daughter-in-law,' said the king.

Dyumatsena was taken aback. 'I am honoured by you request,' said he. 'But we are poor people, who live in the forest. How will your daughter put up with such hardships?' The king assured him that Savitri would be happy to stay in the forest and the matter was settled.

All the sages who lived in the forest knew Satyavan and Savitri. With great eagerness, they arrived at Dyumatsena's ashram and attended the wedding. After the ceremony, the king, queen, all the Brahmanas and pundits took leave and returned to their kingdom. Savitri stayed back in the forest. She discarded her royal robes and dressed as an ascetic in saffron-coloured clothes. She spent her time looking after the needs of her husband and her parents-in-law.

Savitri and Satyavan would meditate together and do all their chores together. They were happy, and the days flew by. Savitri did not forget Narada's prophecy for a single minute. By the end of the year, Savitri grew very anxious. She would count the days. And when there were four days left for the year to end, Savitri gave up food and sleep and spent all her time meditating. Finally the day arrived when Satyavan was supposed to die.

Savitri woke up early and said her prayers. She refused to eat anything before sunset. Soon Satyavan took his axe and was about to leave for the forest when Savitri stopped him. 'I will not let you go alone today. Take me along with you,' she said.

They went to the forest together. The forest looked beautiful. There were ducks swimming in the river, birds twittering on the trees. Satyavan's heart was filled with joy. 'Look Savitri!' he would say, pointing to some squirrel. But Savitri was lost in thought and was unable to enjoy the beauty around her. Her only thought was when that unfortunate moment would arrive.

Soon it was afternoon. They had filled their baskets with fruits. Satyavan started chopping some wood. Suddenly he said, 'Savitri, I am feeling very tired and I have a splitting headache. I want to lie down for some time.' Savitri remembered Narada's prophecy, but she remained very calm. She made Satyavan lie down with his head on her lap and sat very still. A little later, Savitri saw the silhouette of a huge man approaching them. Very soon he was in sight. He looked alarming—with his blood-shot eyes, black body, and red clothes. He was carrying a net in his hand.

Savitri's heart sank when she saw this terrifying man. Politely, she asked the stranger who he was and what he wanted.

'I am Yama, the god of death,' replied the man. 'Satyavan's days on earth are over. I have come here to take him away.'

'But I have heard that it is your messengers' task to take away the dead. Why have you come here yourself?' asked Savitri.

'Satyavan is an exceptional man. He has done many good deeds in his life. That is why I have come personally to fetch him,' replied Yama. Saying this, Yama bent down, and with the help of his net extracted a man the size of a thumb from Satyavan's body. It was Satyavan's soul. Satyavan's body grew limp and lifeless after the extraction of his soul.

With Satyavan's soul tied firmly in the net, Yama started walking towards the north. Savitri followed him in a dazed manner. 'Why are you following me?' asked Yama. 'Don't you have to go back and make preparations for Satyavan's funeral?'

'A wife has to be with her husband,' replied Savitri. 'I have attained the power to go anywhere, with the help of meditation. I want to accompany my husband wherever he goes.'

'Go back Savitri,' said Yama. 'I am impressed by your devotion to your husband. You can ask for a wish. Only don't ask me to bring Satyavan back to life.'

'My father-in-law has lost his eyesight and his kingdom,' replied Savitri. 'He lives in the forest. Please grant him back his vision and his kingdom.'

'So be it,' said Yama. 'I can see that you are quite tired. Please go back home.'

'I am happy to be with my husband,' replied Savitri. 'And am honoured to accompany you. I don't wish to return home.'

'Your words are charming,' said Yama. 'Ask for one more wish.'

Savitri said, 'My father has no sons. Please bless him with a hundred sons.' Yama promised her that this wish, too, would be fulfilled.

'You are Dharma, the god of justice,' said Savitri. 'You are the one who decides who shall be punished or rewarded. And you are merciful to all, including your enemies.'

Yama was so pleased with her that he asked her to make one more wish. 'I wish that Satyavan has a hundred sons,' replied Savitri. Without thinking, Yama granted her this wish. Savitri smiled and said,

'How can Satyavan have a hundred sons if you take him away?'

Yama gladly accepted defeat. He released Satyavan's soul and said, 'You can have Satyavan back. May the two of you live for four hundred years and have a hundred sons!' Yama departed and Savitri went back into the forest. She found Satyavan lying on the ground as she had left him there. Lovingly, she placed Satyavan's head on her lap and he opened his eyes.

'I've been sleeping all these hours!' exclaimed Satyavan, when he was fully awake. 'Why didn't you wake me up? And where is the dark man who was dragging me along?'

'He has gone away,' replied Savitri. 'You seem to be better. Look, it's getting dark. We have to hurry back home.'

And when they reached home, can you guess what they found? Dyumatsena had got back his eyesight. Everyone was relieved to hear that Satyavan was safe. And while they were celebrating, some people from Salva came to visit them. They were Dyumatsena's subjects. They said that their prime minister had defeated the enemies, and that the people of Salva wanted Dyumatsena to return to Salva and rule over them.

So this is where the story ends. Dyumatṣena became the king of Salva again. Satyavan became a prince. Everyone lived happily, and Savitri had a hundred sons.

THE STORY OF NALA AND DAMAYANTI

Prince Nala, who was the ruler of the Nishadhas, was handsome and talented. However, he had one weakness. He loved to gamble. He could not resist a game of dice although he had no skills required for the game.

Damayanti was the daughter of Bhima, the king of Vidarbha. She was extremely beautiful. Nala and Damayanti had heard a lot about each other and felt drawn towards one another, although they had never actually met. One day Nala went out hunting and caught a swan. Just as he was about to kill it, the swan said, 'If you set me free, I shall fly to Damayanti and tell her how handsome you are.' Nala was happy to set the swan free. The swan flew to Damayanti, sang Nala's praises to her, and returned to Nala with a message of Damayanti's love.

Damayanti grew pale and thin, as she pined for Nala. Her father realised that it was time to get his daughter married. He made arrangements for a swayamvara so that Damayanti could choose her husband. The news of Damayanti's swayamvara travelled far and wide. It even reached Indraloka, the dwelling place of the gods. The gods had heard of Damayanti's incredible beauty. Indra, Agni, Yama, and Varuna—the gods of thunder, fire, death, and water—decided to attend the swayamvara and try to win her over. They came down to the earth in their flying machines. They saw Nala ahead of them, on his way to Vidarbha. They called him and asked him to convey the message to Damayanti that they were on their way and that she should choose one of them.

The gods magically transported Nala to an arbour where Damayanti was sitting alone. She was thinking of Nala. She recognised him at first sight. Nala and Damayanti fell in love with each other. Nala conveyed the message of the gods, but Damayanti assured him that she would choose him as her husband and not any of the gods.

When she appeared at the swayamvara, Damayanti was glowing with beauty. The suitors were lined up and Damayanti was alarmed to see that there was not one Nala, but five of them! The four gods had disguised themselves as Nala, hoping to trick her into choosing one of them.

Damayanti did not know what to do. She stood there speechless and unable to move. All she could do was to pray to god and ask him for guidance. The suitors got very puzzled and wondered if she was ill. The four gods realised the depth of her love for Nala. They took pity on her and transformed themselves back to their original forms. Damayanti was much relieved. She continued with the ceremony and chose Nala as her husband.

The gods were so touched by the young couple's devotion to each other that they gave Nala eight special powers as a wedding gift. Indra gave him the speed of a god and the ability to recognise a god when he saw one. Agni gave him the power to create fire when he wanted and the ability to light up dark places. Yama gave him expertise in the art of cooking and the strength to resist temptation. And with Varuna's blessings Nala could magically obtain water and fresh blooms from the most withered plants.

The wedding was conducted on a grand scale. Nala took Damayanti back home. They were very happy together for some time. But their happiness was short-lived. Now, Nala had a brother named Pushkara, who had none of Nala's virtues, and was ambitious and cruel. One day he invited Nala to a game of dice. They played and Nala started losing each game. However, he would not accept defeat. He kept raising his stakes at every throw of the dice, paying no attention to his friends who begged him to stop playing.

Slowly Nala gambled away all his wealth—all his palaces, his elephants, horses, and then finally his kingdom. Pushkara then commanded Nala to stake Damayanti. This shocked Nala and brought him back to his senses. He finally understood how stupid he had been. He left with Damayanti, leaving the kingdom to his brother.

Nala and Damayanti were forced to take refuge in the wild forest. They had to sleep on the ground and satisfy their hunger with berries and even leaves. Nala implored his wife to go back to her father's palace, but Damayanti would not listen to him.

One night, while Damayanti slept under a thorn bush, Nala lay awake. He felt so anxious and helpless that he decided that it would be best for Damayanti if he left her and went away. Quietly, he got up and stole away into the shadows. By the time Damayanti woke up, Nala was far away.

Damayanti burst into tears when she discovered that Nala had deserted her. She did not know what to do. She wandered helplessly through wild forests and narrowly escaped death several times. The gods gave her special powers with the help of which she was able to protect herself from a monstrous snake and a herd of elephants, which came trampling through the forests.

Finally, some kind Brahmans from the kingdom of Chedi found her and took her to their queen mother. The kind lady believed Damayanti's story. She could make out that Damayanti belonged to a good family and was intelligent, even though her skin was scratched and she wore tattered clothes. She took her into her protection and sent messengers to hunt for Nala, who had deserted Damayanti in such a cruel manner.

But where was Nala? He was still in the forest, wandering aimlessly. He was remorseful and in deep despair. He could not believe that he had behaved in such a manner, that he had gambled away his kingdom and then abandoned his wife.

One day he smelt smoke and heard a rustling sound. It was a massive forest fire. As he wondered about what direction to take, he heard a voice crying out for help. 'I am the king of serpents,' said the voice. 'I have been condemned by Narada to lie here till Nala passes by. If you save me, I promise to help you in return.'

Nala found the snake in the undergrowth. It had shrunk to the size of his thumb. He picked it up, covering his mouth and rubbing his eyes as the smoke surrounded him. And then, to his horror, the snake bit him. He was instantly transformed into an ugly, hunch-backed figure. His face was now pock-marked, and he also developed a squint. 'Is this the way to thank me?' he shouted. Calmly the snake replied, 'I have done this to help you. Things will turn out well in the end. You will be handsome once more and will be reunited with your lovely wife. But you must first go to Ayodhya and ask Rituparna, the king of Ayodhya, to appoint you as his charioteer. Teach him horsemanship and he will show you how to win at a game of dice, after which you will be able to win back your kingdom.'

A puzzled Nala followed the serpent's advice. He went to Ayodhya and displayed his swiftness (a gift which he had received from Indra). The king was impressed and appointed him as his charioteer. Soon he was taking lessons in horsemanship from Nala, in spite of his deformities.

Meanwhile, Damayanti's father had sent four Brahmanas to search all over for Nala and Damayanti. Soon they were in Chedi. They recognised Damayanti, although she was now pale and thin. Damayanti revealed her identity to the queen mother, who was delighted because Bhima's wife was her own sister.

Damayanti went back to her father's palace. Her father was happy that she was safe. Damayanti begged her father not to think ill of Nala. After all, it was his evil brother Pushkara who had tempted him to play the game of dice. And, perhaps, in the forest some evil spirit had carried him away. Damayanti was sure that there was some explanation for Nala's behaviour, just that Nala had to be found first.

Damayanti's father agreed to send the Brahmanas out again. They were instructed to ask wherever they went, 'Is there a gambler here, who has abandoned his wife in the forest?'

The Brahmanas returned a few months later. They had found no one who had done such a thing.

However, in the court of King Rituparna, a hideously deformed charioteer called Vahuka had reacted very strangely when the question was asked. He groaned and hastily left the room, clutching his heart and wiping tears from his eyes. But the hideous charioteer could not be Nala, as Nala was more handsome than anyone on earth. Damayanti concluded that the charioteer had some information about Nala. She had to think of a way to bring him to her.

Damayanti went to her father and said that she wished to marry again, since Nala could not be found. She asked him to hold another swayamvara for her. The king was very pleased with her good sense and was happy to announce the swayamvara. Messengers were sent out. They also visited Ayodhya. Rituparna had heard of Damayanti's beauty. He decided to seek her hand.

Nala was to drive Rituparna to the swayamvara. You can imagine how sad he must have felt. He wondered what had driven Damayanti to do this. Maybe her suffering had destroyed her love for him. She would see him at the swayamvara and yet never recognise him as her husband, whom she had once adored.

Nala drove Rituparna to the swayamvara. Their chariot flew with the speed of wind, as Nala had received this power from Indra as a gift. Rituparna was feeling very pleased with Nala. He was also confident of winning Damayanti's hand. He started showing off his knowledge of numbers to Nala. 'Will you teach me how to play dice?' asked Nala, and Rituparna happily agreed.

Soon they arrived at Bhima's court. When Damayanti saw the hideously deformed charioteer, she could not believe that he would know anything about her husband. She asked one of her maids to keep him under close observation.

The maids had astonishing tales to relate bout Vahuka—that he could fill a cup with water with a mere touch, and could light a fire with a wave of his hand. She also said that a bunch of withered flowers had suddenly bloomed when Vahuka had picked them up. Damayanti remembered that these were the gifts that the gods had given Nala at their wedding. Could this man be Nala himself? She asked the maid to take some cooking ingredients to Nala and ask him to prepare a dish with them. When Damayanti tasted the dish that Nala had prepared, she was convinced that Vahuka was her husband.

She called Vahuka and spoke to him directly. 'Did you ever leave your wife in the forest?' she asked. Vahuka replied with tears in his eyes. 'It was me, but it was not my doing. An evil spirit took hold of me, made me gamble away my kingdom, and then made me abandon my wife. You did the right thing by arranging this swayamvara to choose a man worthier than me. Lord Rituparna is here. He is noble and handsome. He will make you very happy.'

But Damayanti said, 'I do not need a swayamvara. You are my husband and I shall go back with you. It does not matter that you have changed in appearance. I also understand that you acted under the influence of the evil spirit. The swayamvara was only a means to bring you here because I knew you would be the one to drive Rituparna here.'

And there was heavenly music in the sky. Petals of flowers fell on Damayanti and Vahuka. As they embraced, Vahuka was transformed once again to the handsome Nala.

Everyone rejoiced when the couple was reunited. Rituparna was also very happy for them. He was true to his promise, and as a wedding gift he taught Nala how to play dice. Nala and Damayanti returned to the kingdom of the Nisadhas. Nala's cruel brother Pushkara was not happy to see them. 'Why are you here?' he asked them. 'This is my kingdom. You lost it all to me. The forest is now your home.'

'Play with me again,' said Nala. 'This time Damayanti will be at stake. If you lose the game, you will return my kingdom to me. But if you win, Damayanti shall be yours and I will have nothing left in the world.'

Pushkara was filled with lust for Damayanti. He was so confident of victory that he agreed to play. The die was cast and Nala won the game because Rituparna had taught him well. Defeated and furious, Pushkara stormed out of the court, vowing to return with an army. But Nala was kind. He called him back and treated him with mercy. He made arrangements for his stay in another part of the kingdom, where he lived quietly for the rest of his life. And Nala and Damayanti lived in contentment.

THE STORY OF DUSHYANTA AND SHAKUNTALA

Have you ever heard of a mother who can abandon her child? There was an Apsara (or a heavenly dancer) who did just that. She left her daughter (who was an infant) by the riverside and simply walked away.

The child was so pretty that the birds of the forest fell in love with her. These birds did not know what to feed a human child. They would sit in a circle around her and keep her protected. They would also raise their wings to shield her from the scorching sunlight.

One day a sage named Kanwa came to the riverside for a bath. When he saw the baby, he picked her up and took her to his ashram. There he brought her up as his own daughter and named her Shakuntala (Shakun means 'bird' in Sanskrit). Shakuntala grew up thinking that Kanwa was her father.

The sage was very happy to have found Shakuntala. Gazing at her face would bring him tremendous joy. Shakuntala was a very bright child. As she grew up, she would run about the ashram and fetch flowers for the sage. All the deer and the birds of the forest were her friends. She would feed them, pet them, and play with them.

Many years went by. Shakuntala grew up into a beautiful woman who had not met too many people. One day Dushyanta, the king of Hastina, came to hunt deer in the forest. He had brought with him a large entourage. The animals in the forest were alarmed by the din created by these men. The king killed many pigs and deer, and would have killed more had he not started feeling extremely thirsty.

He searched all over the forest for water and finally reached Sage Kanwa's ashram. The ashram was lovely. Set deep in the forest, the air around it was filled with the scent of flowers and the humming of birds. The river Malini made a gurgling sound as it flowed past the ashram. The river had many water birds, which made a splashing sound as they swam about in the river.

The king and his men were filled with awe and reverence when they saw the beauty of the ashram. The soldiers felt that they were too dirty to enter the holy place. The king took off his royal robes and entered the hermitage, looking like a common man. King Dushyanta had expected to find Sage Kanwa or some of his pupils in the hermitage. But he was taken aback to find Shakuntala there.

Shakuntala was also surprised to see Dushyanta. She was an intelligent girl and at once understood that Dushyanta was no less than a king, and since Kanwa was not there, she would have to make him feel welcome. She gave him a mat to sit on and some water to wash his face. In a sweet voice, she asked him the purpose of his visit.

'I have come to seek Sage Kanwa's blessings,' said Dushyanta. 'He has gone to get some flowers,' said Shakuntala. 'Please make yourself comfortable.'

King Dushyanta was smitten by Shakuntala's beauty. And when he saw that she was so sweet natured, he could not contain his curiosity. 'Who are you and why do you live in the forest?' he asked very bluntly.

'Sage Kanwa is like a father to me,' replied Shakuntala. 'I have heard that my actual father's name is Vishwamitra and that my mother is Menaka. Sage Kanwa found me on the bank of the river Malini. He has brought me up as his daughter. My name is Shakuntala.'

'I have fallen in love with you, Shakuntala,' said the king. 'Be my queen. I shall dress you up in golden sarees and adorn you with beautiful pearls. I shall travel all over the world to find the rarest of gems for you.'

Shakuntala said that even she had fallen in love with him, and accepted his offer. Shakuntala and Dushyanta exchanged garlands and got married in the Gandharva style. A little later, the king said, 'Shakuntala, please wait for two days. I wish to go back and return with my entire army to receive you.'

Dushyanta left after saying these words. Shakuntala waited patiently for him to return. At this point of time, Sage Kanwa returned to the ashram carrying fruits. Now Sage Kanwa was omniscient, which means that he knew everything about the past, present and the future. So he knew that Shakuntala and Dushyanta had got married. He was very pleased because Dushyanta was kind and noble and was just the sort of man he wanted for Shakuntala. He blessed Shakuntala as soon as he entered the ashram. 'I am very happy for you,' he said. 'You could not have found a man better than Dushyanta. May you have a son who will be the bravest amongst the brave and rule over the entire earth.'

Shakutala's son was born. With Maharishi Kanwa's blessings, he was fearless and brave. At the age of six, he would capture lions, tigers, and elephants, and tie them to tree trunks and give them a good beating! The sages in the forest named him Sarvadaman, or someone who dominates others.

But the strange thing is that Dushyanta did not return. Six years went by. Every day Shakuntala's gaze would follow the path that Dushyanta had taken. 'He will come back today,' she would say to herself, but there were no signs of the king. Shakuntala kept this as a secret because she did not want the others to think ill of her husband.

But why did Dushyanta behave in such a manner? The following incidents that took place led Dushyanta to forget all about his wife:

A few days after Dushyanta left, Sage Durvasa came to to visit Kanwa. Kanwa was not at home.

Shakuntala was so deeply immersed in the thoughts of Dushyanta that she did not notice Durvasa's presence. Durvasa felt so insulted that he cursed Shakuntala. 'Thoughts of Dushyanta have caused you to neglect your duty towards me. May the same Dushyanta forget all about you!' This is the reason why Dushyanta did not return.

When Shakuntala's son was six years old, Sage Kanwa said to her, 'Your son is very brave. He should now be crowned as the Yuvraj or heir to the throne. Take him with you to Hastina.'

Kanwa's words made Shakuntala very happy. But she was also afraid. Quickly she made preparations for the journey. A sage's daughter has very few personal belongings. There was one object that she valued the most. It was a ring that Dushyanta had presented to her at the time of their wedding. She made sure that she had it on her finger, and then packed all her other belongings.

She took two of Kanwa's disciples and, along with her son, made way towards Hastina. Bidding farewell to Kanwa was very painful. However, she thought of her son's future and held back her tears. Shakuntala had so many thoughts to occupy her mind that she paid no attention to the discomforts of the long journey. Her son's questions would interrupt her chain of thoughts, and she would answer him in an absent-minded manner.

Finally they reached Hastina. Kanwa's disciples left her at Dushyanta's court and went back to the forest. But alas! Dushyanta was not overjoyed to see Shakuntala, as she had expected him to be. In fact, he did not even recognise her. Dushyanta looked at Shakuntala and wondered why the unfamiliar woman was staring at him in that manner. It was all very shameful because Shakuntala had to introduce herself. Dushyanta was quite surprised. 'I do not remember meeting you,' he said to her.

At this point Shakuntala broke down. Her head started reeling and she lost consciousness. People in the court rushed to fetch water. Some of them fanned her face. When she came back to her senses, the first thing that came to her mind was the ring. She thought that Dushyanta would remember everything once he saw the ring. However, there was more misfortune in store for her because the ring was not on her finger. She had lost it while washing her face at a stream on her way to Hastina!

With great sadness, Shakuntala said to Dushyanta, 'I am really very unfortunate. My mother abandoned me when I was a child. Now my husband refuses to recognise me. I can always find refuge in my father's ashram. But you are doing your son an injustice by not acknowledging him.'

'I have heard that women are untruthful,' said Dushyanta. 'Maybe you are lying.' Shakuntala was furious. 'I shall go away if you keep insulting me in this manner. But you must remember one thing. My son will rule over the earth after you die.'

The gods, who had been watching everything with mounting impatience, now spoke to Dushyanta. 'Shakuntala is your queen,' they said to him from heaven. 'And this is your own child. Do not abuse Shakuntala any more. Accept both of them with love. Name your son Bharata. He will be a great king one day.'

After the gods had spoken to him, Dushyanta remembered everything in a flash. The people in the king's court had been viewing all the events with great fascination. They were very happy when Dushyanta and Shakuntala were reunited.

Amidst all the merriment, the king's guards brought a fisherman to the king's court. 'This man stole your majesty's ring and was found selling it at the market-place,' they said.

In a trembling voice, the fisherman defended himself. 'Believe me, your majesty,' he said. 'I did not steal your ring. I found it inside the tummy of a fish that I had caught. I didn't know that the ring was yours.'

The ring was passed around. It was obvious that the ring belonged to the king because it had his name written on it. When Dushyanta held it, he recognised it at once as the ring that he had presented to Shakuntala.

Now that everything was explained, you can imagine how happy everyone was. Shakuntala became the queen of Hastina, and Sarvadaman was crowned the prince. He was renamed Bharata. It is not known whether Bharata continued to catch elephants and tigers, but it is very well known that he defeated all his enemies and became a mighty king. India was named Bharat after him.

THE FINAL JOURNEY

This is an unforgettable story from the great epic *Mahabharata*. This is how it goes:

The battle of Kurukshetra had been won by the Pandavas and they ruled over the kingdom for thirty-six years. When they grew old and weak, they handed over their kingdom to a successor and, along with Draupadi, headed towards the northern mountains. Their plan was to end their lives by climbing up to heaven!

It was a long journey. They travelled through many wild forests and over many craggy mountain peaks. As they climbed higher, the air got thinner. They were too old to take the strain. One by one, all the brothers and Draupadi collapsed and died. Yudhishthira was the only survivor because his heart was pure and untouched by sin. He was accompanied by a dog, which had faithfully followed him throughout the journey.

Yudhishthira did not have the means to cremate his brothers and Draupadi or to carry out their last rites. So he left each body where it lay and walked on without a backward glance. He went through forests, over mountains, and across rivers. He reached places which were unexplored by men, and the dog kept following him, although it was old and frail.

All of a sudden he saw Indra, the king of gods, in front of him, riding his golden chariot. 'Noble Yudhishthira,' said he. 'You are the most virtuous amongst men. You have walked far enough. Allow me to take you to heaven in my chariot.'

With great respect and humility, Yudhishthira declined the offer. 'It would not be right for me to enter heaven without my brothers and the queen. They have endured greater hardships than I have. I shall continue walking till my end comes, as it did for them.'

'Do not think that you will reach heaven faster than them,' said Indra. 'Although you left their bodies behind, their souls have already reached heaven, and if you come with me now, you will meet them there.'

Yudhishthira agreed to Indra's request, but he also wanted his dog to go with him. 'He is thin and weak and has followed me so faithfully all this way. I cannot abandon him here in this freezing cold.'

He climbed onto Indra's chariot and beckoned his dog to do the same. The dog wagged his tail and was about to follow him in when Indra stepped forward and stopped the dog. 'This dog is filthy!' he said. 'He will pollute my chariot and contaminate heaven when he reaches there. I cannot allow him in!'

'I do not wish to reach heaven in that case,' said Yudhishthira. 'I would rather die on the mountain-side along with my dog than abandon him, who has been so faithful to me.'

When he heard Yudhishthira's reply, Indra smiled with such warmth that the weather changed and everything looked sunny and cheerful again! 'Well done!' he said. 'You have passed the most difficult test. You placed friendship and loyalty above your desire to reach heaven. Look, your dog is also delighted!'

Yudhishthira turned around and found that his dog was no longer there. Instead, there was his own father Dharma, the god of justice, smiling at him with great pride and warmth. 'It was me following you and not a dog,' said Dharma. 'Your loyalty has made me very happy. Dear son, I bless you for your courage and kindness. Let us now ride to heaven in Indra's chariot, away from the suffering of this world.'

Yudhishthira embraced his father and sat in the chariot. Together they made their journey to heaven. But this is not the end of the story. When Yudhishthira arrived at the gates of heaven, he could not find his brothers, Draupadi, or his allies there. Instead, he saw the souls of his enemies. When he asked where his brothers were, he was told that they were in hell. Once again Yudhishthira refused to enter heaven and demanded to be taken to hell.

The chariot took him down to hell. He was very sad to find that his brothers and Draupadi were being tortured there. He heard their screams of agony. 'I do not understand how this could have happened,' he said to Indra. 'Our enemies are in heaven and we have been condemned to stay in hell. However, if this is what the gods desire, I accept it.'

'O noble king!' said Indra. 'You have passed the ultimate test. The heaven and hell that you saw were a mirage. You were not entirely without sin. That is why you needed a glimpse of hell. But now that you have atoned fully for your weaknesses, you shall enter the real heaven. May you be reunited with your brothers and queen and receive the honour that you deserve.'

Yudhishthira found himself at the gates of the true heaven this time. As Indra's chariot flew through the gates of heaven, Yudhishthira left his body behind and turned to pure soul. When he reached heaven, he was welcomed by his brothers, the queen, and his divine father Dharma.

